The Privacy Debate

Editor: Tracy Biram

Volume 383

independence
educational publishers

First published by Independence Educational Publishers

The Studio, High Green

Great Shelford

Cambridge CB22 5EG

England

© Independence 2021

Copyright

Photocopy licence

ISBN-13: 978 1 86168 841 5

Printed in Great Britain

Zenith Print Group

Contents

Introduction

The Prvacy Debate is Volume 383 in the **issues** series. The aim of the series is to offer current, diverse information about important issues in our world, from a UK perspective.

ABOUT THE PRIVACY DEBATE

Privacy is a fundamental human right. In modern society the capabilities to protect our privacy are greater than ever, yet, so are the capabilities to compromise that privacy. This book looks at the rise of surveillance technology, the ways in which privacy can be invaded without our knowledge and the laws created to protect us. It also examines the issue of 'sharenting' – breaching children's privacy by posting photos of them on social media without their consent.

OUR SOURCES

Titles in the **issues** series are designed to function as educational resource books, providing a balanced overview of a specific subject.

The information in our books is comprised of facts, articles and opinions from many different sources, including:

- Newspaper reports and opinion pieces
- Website factsheets
- Magazine and journal articles
- Statistics and surveys
- Government reports
- Literature from special interest groups.

A NOTE ON CRITICAL EVALUATION

Because the information reprinted here is from a number of different sources, readers should bear in mind the origin of the text and whether the source is likely to have a particular bias when presenting information (or when conducting their research). It is hoped that, as you read about the many aspects of the issues explored in this book, you will critically evaluate the information presented.

It is important that you decide whether you are being presented with facts or opinions. Does the writer give a biased or unbiased report? If an opinion is being expressed, do you agree with the writer? Is there potential bias to the 'facts' or statistics behind an article?

ASSIGNMENTS

In the back of this book, you will find a selection of assignments designed to help you engage with the articles you have been reading and to explore your own opinions. Some tasks will take longer than others and there is a mixture of design, writing and research-based activities that you can complete alone or in a group.

FURTHER RESEARCH

At the end of each article we have listed its source and a website that you can visit if you would like to conduct your own research. Please remember to critically evaluate any sources that you consult and consider whether the information you are viewing is accurate and unbiased.

Useful Websites

www.aljazeera.com

www.bigbrotherwatch.org.uk

www.grcworldforums.com

www.independent.co.uk

www.inews.co.uk

www.medium.com

www.medium.designit.com

www.newstatesman.com

www.privacyinternational.org

www.robbreport.co.uk

www.theconversation.com

www.theguardian.com

uk.pcmag.com

www.videosurveillance.blog.gov.uk

The data protection and privacy trends to watch out for in 2021

PrivSec Report looks forward to the new year and what it could mean for the privacy and data protection worlds.

By Catherine Wycherely

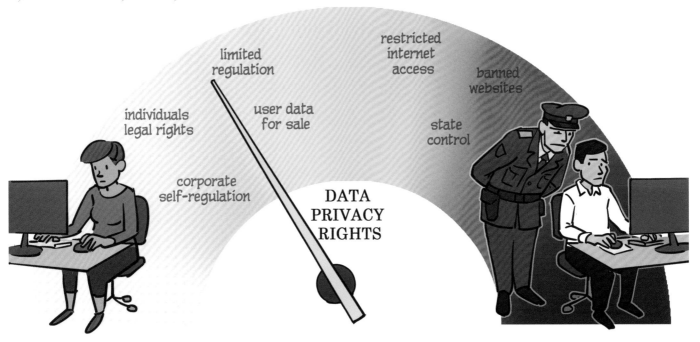

Here are the key topics and trends we expect to see in 2021:

1. Privacy culture for all, as public awareness grows

2020 has been defined by the global pandemic which has affected every part of the world, every sector, every business, and every individual. But 2020 has not only ushered in an unexpected lay grounding in epidemiology, it has also seen a continued growth in consumer awareness of privacy rights, both driven by and reflected in an explosion of privacy and data protection regulation across the globe, even as Covid-19 spread.

With the publicising of issues such as location and health-related data collection and the growing need for employers to handle health-related employee data, privacy has an assured place in the spotlight through to 2021.

Some, like Camilla Winlo, Director of Consultancy at data protection and privacy consultancy DQM GRC, believe that the combination of consumer awareness and regulation will turn a spotlight on data ethics as a driver for decision making in 2021.

"Organisations will explicitly link their corporate vision and values to their ethical position around privacy and data protection, and we will increasingly see data ethics and privacy as a theme within annual reports and internal communications," says Winlo.

As the privacy landscape evolves, and DPOs and CPOs continue to feel the weight of the task ahead of them, next year could also see a developing realisation that security and privacy need to work hand-in-hand in this brave new world.

"That connectivity with data governance and security has been there in the more mature areas for a little while, and it's now openly talked about," says Victoria Guilloit, Partner at consultancy Privacy Culture. That could manifest, she suggests, with more CISOs and CPOs reporting into a Chief Data Officer, with the CPO retaining an alliance with legal and the CISO with IT. More implementation of this role could have the potential to balance the budget between the often under-resourced privacy department, and the more established and better financed security team.

"I'd say it's like we're in high school just about understanding that we need to have solid partnerships with our data governance partners, with our security teams – really understand that collaboration," adds Heather Federman, VP of Privacy and Policy at BigID.

2. The privacy landscape will increase in complexity

Gartner predicts that 65% of people across the world will have their personal data protected by privacy regulations, compared to 10% in 2020. New data protection regimes are in the pipeline, such as China, which in October published a first draft of its comprehensive Personal Information Protection Law (Draft PIPL), aiming to protect the personal data of residents of mainland China, and Australia, which is currently consulting on changes to its privacy legislation.

India's Personal Data Protection Bill, introduced in 2019, is currently pending consideration after being delayed by Covid-19, and has similarities with the GDPR, as well as crucial differences that some privacy commentators have concerns about.

"On the one hand, India is trying to make itself this new tech hub of the world, competing with China, and they have this draft bill. But on the other hand, there's some really ambiguous and onerous provisions in that bill as well that go beyond what GDPR does and give the government much more authority over citizens' data and companies' data than I think others would like," says Federman.

"That to me is probably the biggest one just because of how central a part India plays within the tech supply chain world," she adds.

For companies operating internationally, the need to juggle multiple regulatory frameworks will continue into 2021 and beyond. Undoubtedly, the GDPR continues to cast a global shadow, influencing both emerging data protection frameworks and reasonably mature ones, such as the DIFC, which recently updated its 2007 law to be more aligned with the GDPR.

This ripple is likely to continue, and organisations subject to regimes like the GDPR or California's CCPA may find it expedient to roll out those protections even outside the jurisdictions covered by those laws.

In the US, for example, without a federal privacy law at present, Sheryl Falk, Partner and co-leader of Winston & Strawn's Global Privacy and Data Security practice, says:

"I predict that more and more companies will consider expanding data privacy rights beyond the required jurisdictions (California, Nevada, and the EU) in order to streamline data privacy rights requests and to be seen as good corporate citizens."

3. The debate over a federal privacy law in the US will rumble on

Whether or not the US will exchange (or supplement) its patchwork of state and sector level privacy and data protection regulations for a comprehensive federal law, remains anyone's guess.

Falk is optimistic: "I predict that in 2021, we may finally see the long-awaited federal privacy law, which would address how companies handle consumer data. The political will and momentum from a change in administration increases the likelihood of passage," she says.

"This new law would likely follow the California model focusing on transparency and consumer rights (as opposed to the European framework)."

Federman, on the other hand, is "deeply cynical" of the federal wrangle being solved in 2021.

With uncertainty lingering into January over control of the Senate, the lack of a bipartisan consensus on the nature of any federal legislation – largely over federal pre-emption and private right of action – is likely to persist, at least in the short term. That's not to say, however, that legislation won't continue to proliferate at the state level next year, as other states catch up not only with California's trailblazing CCPA, but its newly passed California Consumer Privacy Rights Act, set to come into enforcement in 2023.

With questions of technology regulation – both in terms of competition and the responsibility of social media companies over content published on their platforms – still in the headlines, the new administration's stance on tech will be key next year. Certainly Vice-President-Elect Kamala Harris has expressed interest in privacy in the past – "she was one of the first public officials I've ever seen tweet about a privacy issue", says Federman – having created a Privacy Enforcement and Protection Unit in the Department of Justice focused on protecting consumer and individual privacy through civil prosecution of state and federal privacy laws as Attorney General of California, back in 2012.

"Protecting the privacy of Californians is one of Attorney General Harris's top priorities", said the news release at the time.

Whether Biden will build on Obama's amenity towards privacy moves – for example his 2012 Consumer Privacy Bill of Rights – could become clearer next year.

With support on both sides of the political divide and among the business community itself, hopes are high for future US federal legislation – but when? For now, data privacy consultant Debbie Reynolds is modest in her immediate wishlist:

"The thing that I wish would happen, because I think it's like the lowest hanging fruit you could possibly have, is that all 50 states have data breach notification laws, and they're different in every state. If they could come up with the law where it harmonises that across a federal level, I'll be super happy – that would be the first step, maybe that could be a foundation to other things."

4. Uncertainty over international data transfers will persist

Ambiguity over international data transfers has dogged 2020. July saw the Court of Justice of the European Union (CJEU) strike down the Privacy Shield, which previously allowed data transfers between the EU and the US, in part over CJEU concerns about access to data by US surveillance mechanisms.

Solving the Privacy Shield issue could be a pressure point for the incoming US administration, not least because of the importance of data transfers to frustrated US and global businesses.

But it is not just those transacting with the US that will be following the regulatory fall-out of the Schrems II decision into 2021.

October 2020 saw the same court rule that EU privacy rules have jurisdiction over national security rules requiring companies to collect and retain general and indiscriminate bulk communications data with security agencies – with implications for the UK's acquisition and use of communications data by British Security and Intelligence Agencies. The ruling could have significant implications for the UK's bid for adequacy with the GDPR when the post-Brexit transition period ends on 1 January.

Standard Contractual Clauses remain valid for data transfers between the EU and socalled "third countries" (like the US and potentially the UK) under the Schrems II decision, although those wishing to transfer personal data must apply a case-by-case risk analysis to assess the suitability of the recipient country's data projection regime and practice, placing pressure on businesses and regulators. Where shortfalls are identified, supplementary measures may be applied, and the European Data Protection Board (EDPB) is consulting on guidance for data exporters to establish what measures are necessary and effective, such as encryption and pseudonymisation. The EDPB also set out "European Essential Guarantees", for determining whether third country laws allowing access to data for the purposes of surveillance constitute a "justifiable interference" with privacy and personal data protections.

According to Guilloit, however, many people seeking to navigate Brexit in early 2021 "don't feel as if that [supplementary measures] guidance is hugely helpful… people are waiting for a precedent as well."

The feedback period has also just closed on new (and more comprehensive) draft SCCs published by the EU, which are expected to be finalised in Q1, which could bring more clarity. However, Peter Crowther, Managing Partner at Winston & Strawn, and Lisa Hatfield, Associate Attorney, say: "At least at present, a one-year transition period is envisaged within which the existing SCCs may be used in existing unchanged contracts, but it is expected after this period that all business will use the new clauses. This will inevitably cause disruption for businesses which rely on the current versions. Businesses should start to consider this process as soon as possible, not least because the new drafts include various warranties and obligations about third country laws which might affect compliance (following the Schrems decision)."

Amid the uncertainty, data localisation may increasingly rear its head in 2021.

"I expect organisations will think much harder about the reasons why they transfer data outside of its originating country. The perceived risk associated with such transfers is increasing, and the steps necessary to permit such transfers mean that many processes simply won't work in their current format anymore," says Camilla Winlo, at DQM GRC.

Winlo adds that some cross-border transfers may be prevented by supervisory authorities.

She says: "This makes international transfers a business continuity issue – and one that is solved by designing localised alternative processes. Once these localised processes have been finalised, it will become more difficult to justify the continuation of data transfers. Hence, I expect to see an increasing move to localise data processing."

Data professionals will need to have mapped out where their data actually is, be on top of local laws, and completely across contracts. But they will also want to consider whether international transfers are truly necessary.

Nevertheless, organisations should also apply a degree of calm and pragmatism in the current climate, says Guilloit: "Regulators are typically massively underfunded and under-resourced," she says. Given the context of the pandemic, she anticipates limited capacity for a huge regulatory push that could damage businesses as they seek to keep data flowing across borders in early 2021.

"I think there'll be a massive pushback by governments protecting businesses if that happens, saying, come on, we're just recovering from Covid, what are you doing?"

She adds: "I think we might have got a reprieve from Schrems because of Covid."

5. A maturing understanding of the potential for automation among privacy professionals

2020 has not seen an eradication of poor data hygiene, nor the risks associated with unstructured, unclassified, aged and poorly understood gobbets of data lurking on company devices and servers, alongside a lack of standardised processes for processing data across industries. With

Covid-19 driving masses of staff into remote working, the difficulties of data tracking have intensified as use of home networks and BYOD have increased.

Many organisations are still grappling with the development of a (manual or automated) data inventory, and companies face a proliferating choice of solutions for automating the process through data discovery and management.

Federman, at New York-headquartered company BigID, which uses advanced machine learning and identity intelligence to discover and map data, believes the privacy market is at the "infancy" of automation.

Guillot says that the use of automation in the privacy space is less evolved than it could be, and much centres on the ethics of using tech in this way.

"On the security side, it's been there for so long – it's a bit of an in joke in the industry, just buy another box of flashing lights and throw it at it, whereas on the privacy side that that generally at the moment hasn't happened," she says.

"There's a there's a lot of talk about automation in privacy. There's a lot of talk about AI and machine learning, and the pros and cons of that… It can't stop going in that direction, they're not going to stop developing. But, I think typically the people in the privacy space will question whether or not it's right to do it. I think that's the difference."

6. We are unlikely to reach consensus over the use of encryption

October saw the release of a statement from the United States Department of Justice, undersigned by representatives from the US, UK, Australia, New Zealand, Canada, India and Japan, arguing that end-to-end encryption technology poses challenges to public safety, including to highly vulnerable members of society such as sexually exploited children.

The statement called for law enforcement to be allowed to access content in "a readable and usable format where an authorisation is lawfully issued, is necessary and proportionate", and to consult with governments to facilitate legal access.

As of 21 December, the European Electric Communications Code (EECC) removes the explicit legal basis for Over-The-Top (OTT) companies to voluntarily scan online material for child sexual abuse unless national law allows them to do, although a temporary proposal allows voluntary detection of child sexual abuse to continue until 2025.

In a December 2020 report, the UK Children's Commissioner, Anne Longfield, said that end-to-end encryption of electronic communications should not apply to children's accounts with tech companies such as Facebook Messenger. She warned the government to be wary of big tech's intentions around encryption, stating social media firms may be using encryption in a "cynical" attempt to "side-step sanctions and litigation".

But privacy campaigners, such as the Electronic Frontier Foundation, are opposed to any attempts, EU or US-based, to weaken encryption.

"The problem is the solution – that they want to weaken encryption for everybody," says consultant Debbie Reynolds.

"They want to be a given a key so they can unlock the contents of X person's data. But what they're asking for really is to create a vulnerability so they can unlock everybody's data. Once they create their vulnerability, that vulnerability is everywhere."

Any inroads into a softening of end-to-end encryption in 2021 will likely generate vigorous debate between big tech players, regulators and privacy campaigners – not to mention potential complexity over European supplementary SCC measures to enable international data transfers.

17 December 2020

Online privacy is a right, not a luxury

The tech industry is finally waking up to the fact that people care about their privacy. But current solutions all come at too high a cost in money or time to the end user, according to security expert Max Eddy.

By Max Eddy

Weeks after pitching this story to my editor, I had the disorienting experience of seeing a near-identical headline in the New York Times, penned by none other than Google CEO Sundar Pichai. Great minds think alike, it seems, and I believe Pichai is on the right track. By and large people have started to demand better privacy protections for everyone, and even holding companies that fail to protect their privacy to account. The problem is, I don't believe Pichai goes far enough.

When we don't view privacy as a right, it risks becoming a checkbox on a laundry list of features at exorbitant prices. When that happens, the entire industry fails the consumer. Pichai calls for legislation and smarter data-gathering practices, but what we really need is a total overhaul of the internet, led by companies like Apple and Google.

Granted, there's always been a certain connection between wealth and privacy. If you're rich, you can live in a big house with high walls. You can afford to put that house out in the country, far from other people. You can pay for the car, and the gas, and the car insurance to get to and from that house. You could even pay for a high-tech home security system. The difference today is that the wealthy aren't paying for an extra level of privacy, they're paying to not have their privacy eroded further. In security circles, it's often said that "if it's free, you're the product." I think it's more accurate to say that if you can't afford to pay, then you're the product.

Free services, pricey devices

Apple has a hard-earned reputation for security and privacy, particularly on iOS. Despite that, the company long shied away from making privacy and security a major talking point. It would come up now and then, an ad or billboard here and there, but the Apple event in March, 2019 changed that. Privacy was a key talking point for each and every product. I have a collection of screenshots on my desktop of the black screens and white text that read out proclamations like "Apple doesn't allow advertisers to track you" and "Apple doesn't know how much you paid for it."

That's good. I don't want Apple to know those things or let advertisers track me. The implication is, however, that only by paying for Apple products can I access this lifestyle where I'm not tracked and profiled constantly. If I can't afford an iPhone, then I don't get privacy. Or rather, if I can't afford $699 for a now-dated iPhone 8 or (god help me) $999 or more for an iPhone XS, I don't get privacy.

There are many good and worthy Android devices out there, but until the release of the Pixel 3a Google failed to bring robust and affordable smartphones to market. Too often, Android users have to trade away security features, like NFC payments or fingerprint readers, in order to get a phone that would fit within a reasonable budget. Android phones from outside the big G also have major tradeoffs, with manufacturers sometimes delaying the release of important security updates or introducing their own vulnerabilities. I believe that may be changing, but hardcore privacy advocates will tell you that using a Google phone is surrendering any semblance of privacy. In a future column, I'll detail my own comical experiences trying to de-Google an Android phone.

Beyond the hegemony

Perhaps in response to rising anxiety about how much big tech knows about our lives, a new crop of devices designed from the ground up to be open-source and privacy-respecting is on the rise. Purism is a company that offers the Librem line of Linux-based laptops built with privacy and security in mind. As with Apple, however, it comes at a cost.

The Librem laptop starts at around $1,399, which is pricier than Apple's cheapest laptop. Librem is also working to introduce its first smartphone, called the Librem 5. Since it's unreleased, I have no idea if it's any good, but I do know the preorder price is $649, which is less than the newest iPhone but still 50 percent more than the cheapest iPhone, the $499 iPhone 7.

Privacy hardliners occasionally call for consumers to build their own devices, and learn the joys of Linux. This too has a cost, but an invisible one. If you have a problem, you won't be able to go to an Apple store and may not even find documentation online.

Instead, you'll have to trawl through forum posts. If you aren't already comfortable working in the command line, writing your own code, or mucking around in the guts of an operating system you'll have to take the time to learn. And time is money—especially if you're an hourly wage or gig employee. While there are many free or open-source alternatives to major software tools, working on platforms other than industry standard can make your job that much more difficult.

The price of a new computer is already pretty hefty, and adding these invisible costs for the sake of privacy and security is a heavy burden. That's especially true when you can get an excellent Chromebook, brought to you by Google, for $250 and all the private data they can squeeze out of you.

Breaking free of privacy-eroding systems also has a social cost. Not engaging on Facebook, Twitter, and Instagram can mean being cut off from an important way friends and family connect and stay connected. It can also hurt your career. I'm not happy about how Twitter has handled user privacy,

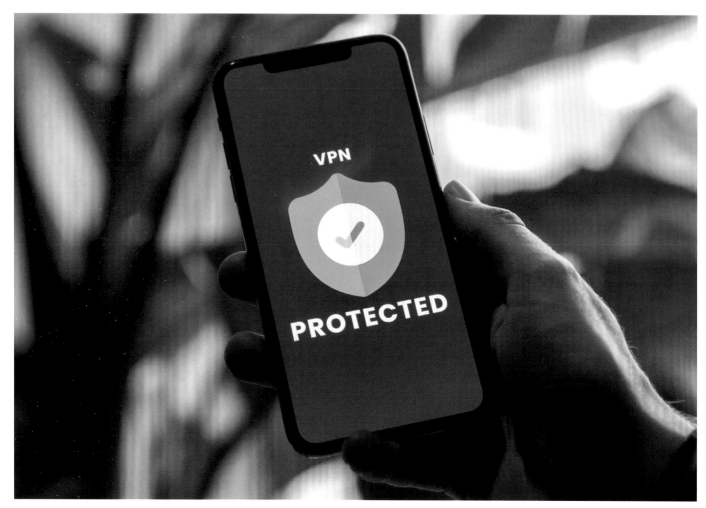

nor with how it allows actual nazis to use its platform, but if I actually quit it altogether I'd lose a valuable avenue for connecting with readers and for spreading my work.

We can't tech our way out

Along with privacy-promoting devices, recent years have also seen a rise in privacy securing software. At least part of the reason why VPNs have become popular is the sense that more people are spying on you, turning your data into money without your knowledge.

Services like Abine Blur and DeleteMe go further. Blur, for a fee, will help you reduce the spread of personal information on the web by letting you hide it behind masked email addresses and disposable prepaid credit card numbers. DeleteMe actively seeks out your information on data broker websites and, again for a fee, works to get that information removed. Taken together, these services can run you well over $150 a year.

While I appreciate that there are companies out there actively seeking to remedy our situation, I believe it is fundamentally unfair that consumers have to pay extra for the privacy that is their right as human beings. It shouldn't be necessary to pay extra to maintain the level of privacy that should be intrinsic to everyone.

Privacy is a right, not a feature

The tech industry is driven heavily by novelty; by building and marketing the thing that everyone suddenly wants. First it was touch-screen phones, then app stores, then (briefly)

3D TV, then (also briefly?) VR, and so on. I fear that privacy has become the next new thing, and instead of fundamentally fixing our devices and infrastructure to assure privacy, we'll simply pay a premium for what should be our right.

As with climate change, corporations and consumers alike benefited from an unsustainable process, and now we have to face the consequences. We can continue down this path, where only the wealthiest will be worthy of remaining untracked by an evergrowing cornucopia of corporations buying and trading our personal information, but it will poison us. Trading personal information for services has had a hand in many of our modern ills: data breaches, mass surveillance, and election interference—to name just a few.

Instead of this toxicity, the corporations that acquired that wealth and the governments that allowed them to flourish need to invest in the systems that made the information age a success. We need devices people can actually afford that won't be subsidized at the expense of their privacy. We need a new internet, built with privacy-securing foundations that will enable a new generation of services and technologies.

I don't know how we get there, but I know that nobody should take what's ours and sell it back to us.

22 May 2019

The future of your privacy: universal right, luxury, commodity or utility

Four scenarios on the future of privacy regulations and their implications.

By Maria Chercoles, co-founder of Grey Area Collective, a research and design think tank

Common sense would suggest that in the wake of Facebook's many scandals, users would be leaving in droves — and yet the network is more popular than ever. Meanwhile, the number of smart speakers worldwide is set to reach 225 million by 2020, despite multiple incidents of speakers recording private conversations and sending them to acquaintances without the user's knowledge. If that sounds eerie, it's just the beginning. Within our lifetimes, we should expect all sorts of technology to become fully embedded into our lives, "watching over" our every decision, conversation and thought.

Last year, the European Union rolled out the General Data Protection Regulation (GDPR) — the largest attempt yet at protecting user data. In the US, federal regulation of that reach has yet to pass, but it hasn't stopped at least 12 states passing their own privacy laws. The 2018 California Consumer Privacy Protection is the strongest of all, guaranteeing users the right to know what data is being collected, and opting out of the sale of their data. However, this kind of regulation is the exception rather than the rule.

And if you look at the opposite end of the scale, the Chinese government is actually collecting personal data from citizens to build a social credit system to incentivize good behavior.

So with governments adopting different positions across the globe, and most users ambivalent about sharing data as long as there's a clear value exchange, what does the future of privacy look like? Inspired by trends, drivers, and news, here are four possible scenarios based on two uncertainties: Who will regulate privacy — governments or tech companies themselves? And how much will the public care about the topic?

Scenario 1: Privacy as a luxury

In this scenario, customers express a clear desire for more privacy, but there is little government intervention. As a result, tech companies take advantage of the free market to charge as much as users are willing to pay for the security guarantee. Transparency and privacy become a competitive feature — delivered at a premium.

Early trends pointing this way include Google's omission of the camera from the Home Hub, and Facebook's "Private by Design" branding campaign for its new Portal device. If this scenario holds true, we can expect more devices with robust privacy safeguards: camera covers, the option to turn off and disconnect listening and face recognition functions, local data storage only, and the ability to seamlessly see and determine what's saved and what's not.

Only the most affluent will have complete control over their privacy, paying monthly fees to use private email accounts, social networks, and other services — while the rest use "free" options that exploit their data.

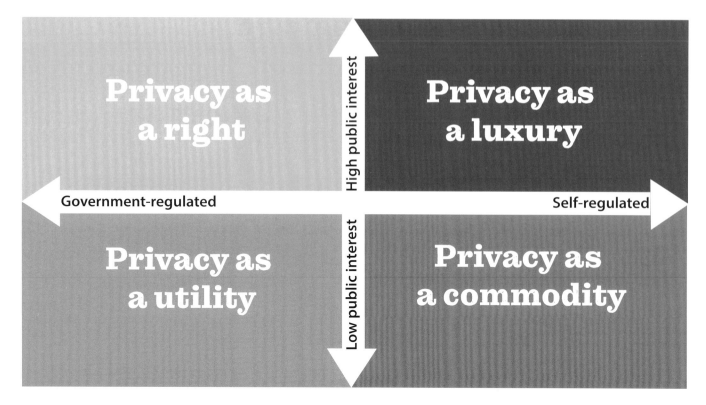

Scenario 2: Privacy as a commodity

In this scenario we find a society in which neither citizens nor governments care about privacy regulation, giving the tech industry total autonomy over data collection, its exchange, and trade. In this free market, people are powerless over what information is being transferred, while tech companies make huge profits by selling data to brands.

All the devices around us, regardless of whether we own them or not, are collecting and sharing information about us. Algorithms anticipate everything from when we'll be hungry to what our child's favorite toy will be next year. Smart speakers in our self-driving cars listen to our conversations so that the digital billboards on the road can be targeted just for us, and the driving route is not the fastest one, but the one that passes by the highest bidding retail store.

In this scenario, we might get the illusion of choice. But our options for what to eat, what to read, what to wear, and where to go will be limited to those presented by companies that pay to be present in our lives.

Scenario 3: Privacy as a utility

Here we find a government committed to protecting citizens' privacy rights, but a society that has grown indifferent. Privacy becomes something governments regulate and monitor, but citizens take it for granted and don't spend a lot of time looking into it, much like power and water regulations.

Devices come with privacy scorecards, similar to energy efficiency rankings on appliances.

These scorecards visualize all the ways the device collects and analyzes data and what it does with it. Is video being recorded? Does it do facial recognition? These numbers might influence a purchase along with beautiful design and sale price, but won't be the key selling point for everyone, and will soon be forgotten once the device is installed. Citizens receive a monthly email statement of their data that's being collected and used, but it will most likely stay unopened or be deleted right away, with most people deciding to opt out of such boring information.

Scenario 4: Privacy as a right

In this scenario, governments heavily regulate privacy laws, driven in part by a public that demands protection. The right to own and control one's data and online persona becomes a fundamental, universal right. Early signals pointing towards this are Europe's GDPR and California's Consumer Privacy Protection laws.

Users have complete visibility and control over all their data. By law, tech giants issue monthly data statements, similar to bank statements, listing all the information they collected from us and how it was used. In addition, users have the power to adjust privacy settings to their level of comfort. All of this free of charge. In full control of what we share and don't share, some people even profit by renting their data to tech companies.

So what will the future of privacy really look like?

None of these scenarios are absolute, nor are they attempts to predict what will happen.

The future of privacy will likely be a combination of these scenarios, but will also be influenced by wild cards, things we can't even imagine today. We should also expect privacy regulation and attitudes around it to be different across different parts of the world.

One thing we can be certain of: our future will be defined by the decisions and actions we make today. Exploring different outcomes helps us think about what kind of future we want — and the steps we need to take to get there.

1 July 2019

Privacy is the ultimate luxury, according to security experts Hunter Protection

The peace of mind it leads to trumps all of life's other offerings, according to a firm whose raison d'être is to protect Royal Families, Heads of State and Diplomats, among others.

By Anya Cooklin-Lofting

Some of life's finest pleasures are harder to spot. Silence is a good example, as is privacy. Less obvious luxuries such as these often make themselves apparent the moment they are taken away. The sudden, persistent ringing of a car alarm outside raises the status of the purest silence to one of precious luxury. More pressingly, the compromising of one's privacy will elucidate the bliss of absolute privacy itself.

Privacy is held as the ultimate luxury by Hunter Protection, a private protection provider to UHNW clients including international Royal families, Heads of State, ultra-high-networth individuals and Fortune 100 CEOs. Its Founder, Karen Connell, believes that privacy and personal safety are intrinsically linked, and works with her team of highly-trained Close Protection Officers, Security Ambassadors and Chauffeurs, each dedicated, discreet and highly professional. The value of privacy is taken so seriously by all personnel at Hunter Protection that this elite team of operatives themselves keep incredibly low profiles. It is only Connell herself that is known to the public as a member of the Hunter Protection team.

Connell has worked in over 42 countries as well as heading up Hunter Protection, and is an expert in communication

and behavioural science. She works personally with Hunter Protection's operatives, training them to build effective and professional relationships quickly so they can keep the 'person' in 'personal security' and maintain clients' privacy, and thus their safety.

One of the primary concerns for safety in the current climate is that of violent crime. As of August, violent crime rates have crept back up to their pre-coronavirus levels and could escalate further as the economy continues to feel the implications of the pandemic. In a recent interview with The Guardian, Sadiq Khan said he believed "There is a real risk of violent crime spiking as lockdown is eased."

"Desperate people do desperate things," says Connell, adding that "Now is the time to feel assured that high-level emergency threat plans are in place to protect your privacy and that of your family." Hunter Protection has continued to protect their clients and their families, homes and businesses throughout this increase in crime levels in London, New York and many other global capitals. She warns that wherever you go, "There are too many security guards who operate with minimum qualifications and experience, and even more homes with alarm systems that are not monitored or functioning properly. This is a huge compromise to the privacy, safety and peace of mind of people all over the world." This is why each of Hunter Protection's operatives is trained to work under exceptional circumstances, anticipating scenarios and outcomes for individuals, families and for corporate personnel. Each Hunter Protection assignment or long-term protection programme involves in-depth planning and logistics to ensure the delivery of the security measures is effective and highly discreet. Hunter Protection's operatives are veterans from the British Elite Forces, British Military Intelligence and Royalty and UHNW Protection.

Their forensic attention to detail, unrivalled expert knowledge and military precision define Hunter Protection's network of protection personnel. With countless operational tours of duty in their portfolios, the officers are personally selected to offer Hunter Protection's clients the ultimate luxuries: privacy, safety and the freedom to relax.

21 August 2020

The privacy paradox: we claim we care about our data, so why don't our actions match?

An article from The Conversation.

By Ivano Bongiovanni (Lecturer in Information Security, Governance and Leadership / Design Thinking, The University of Queensland), Karen Renaud (Visiting Professor, Rhodes University) and Noura Aleisa (Assistant professor of Computer Science, Saudi Electronic University)

THE CONVERSATION

Imagine how you'd feel if you discovered footage from your private home security camera had been broadcast over the internet. This is exactly what happened to several unsuspecting Australians last month, when the website Insecam streamed their personal lives online.

According to an ABC report, Insecam broadcasts live streams of dozens of Australian businesses and homes at any given time. Some cameras can be accessed because owners don't secure them. Some may be hacked into despite being "secured".

When asked if they care about their personal information being shared online, most people say they do. A 2017 survey found 69% of Australians were more concerned about their online privacy than in 2012.

However, a much smaller percentage of people actually take the necessary actions to preserve their privacy. This is referred to as the "privacy paradox", a concept first studied about two decades ago.

To investigate this phenomenon further, we conducted a research project and found that, despite being concerned about privacy, participants were willing to sacrifice some of it in exchange for the convenience afforded by an internet-connected device.

Unpacking the privacy paradox

Any "smart" device connected to the internet is called an Internet of Things (IoT) device. These can be remotely monitored and controlled by the owners.

The projected growth of IoT devices is staggering. By 2025, they're expected to reach 75.44 billion – an increase of 146% from 2020.

Are device owners genuinely concerned about their privacy? Recent worldwide anxiety about personal information shared through COVID-19 tracing apps seems to suggest so.

But as the privacy paradox highlights, users expressing privacy concerns often fail to act in accordance with them. They freely divulge personal information in exchange for services and convenience.

Explanations for the privacy paradox abound. Some suggest:

♦ people find it difficult to associate a specific value to their privacy and therefore, the value of protecting it

♦ people do not consider their personal information to be their own and thus might not appreciate the need to secure it

♦ people completely lack awareness of their right to privacy or privacy issues and believe their desired goals (such as a personalised experience) outweigh the potential risks (such as big tech companies using their data for profiling).

The likely explanation for the privacy paradox is a mix of all these factors.

What if we proved your device harvests data?

To understand whether and how the privacy paradox applies to IoT devices, we conducted an experiment involving 46 Saudi Arabian participants. This is because in Saudi Arabia the use of IoT is exploding and the country does not have strong privacy regulations.

We gave participants a smart plug that let them switch a table lamp on or off using an app on their smartphone. We then showed them the device's privacy policy and measured participants' privacy concerns and trust in the device.

None of the participants read the privacy policy. They simply agreed to commence with the study.

After two hours, we presented evidence of how much of their data the IoT-connected plug was harvesting, then remeasured their privacy concerns and trust.

After the participants saw evidence of privacy violation, their privacy concerns increased and trust in the device decreased. However, their behaviour did not align with their concern, as shown by the fact that:

♦ 15 participants continued to use the device regardless

♦ 13 continued to use it with their personal information removed

♦ only three opted to block all outbound traffic to unusual IP addresses.

The rest preferred "light-touch" responses, such as complaining on social media, complaining to the device's manufacturer or falsifying their shared information.

After one month, we measured participants' attitudes a third time and discovered their privacy concerns and trust in the device had reverted to pre-experiment levels.

How to prevent complacency

Two decades since the first privacy paradox studies were conducted and despite a great deal of research, there is still a mismatch between people's stated privacy concerns and their protective behaviours. How can we improve this?

The first step is to simply be aware our judgement of IoT device risks and benefits may not be accurate. With that in mind, we should always take time to read the privacy policies of our devices.

Besides informing us of the risks, reading privacy policies can help us stop and think before connecting a new device to the internet. Ask yourself: "is this really going to benefit me?"

As citizen surveillance increases, it's not wise to mindlessly scroll through privacy policies, tick a box and move on.

Second, we should not assume our personal information is trivial and would not interest anyone. Time after time we have witnessed how our digital traces can be valuable to malicious individuals or large corporations.

And finally, always change the default password on any new IoT device to a stronger one. Write down this password and secure it, perhaps with other physical valuables, so you don't have to worry about forgetting it.

29 July 2020

Privacy is a collective concern

When we tell companies about ourselves, we give away details about others, too.

By Carissa Véliz

People often give a personal explanation of whether they protect the privacy of their data.

Those who don't care much about privacy might say that they have nothing to hide. Those who do worry about it might say that keeping their personal data safe protects them from being harmed by hackers or unscrupulous companies. Both positions assume that caring about and protecting one's privacy is a personal matter. This is a common misunderstanding.

It's easy to assume that because some data is "personal", protecting it is a private matter.

But privacy is both a personal and a collective affair, because data is rarely used on an individual basis.

Suppose, for example, you buy a DNA testing kit. For about £100, you can hand over a sample of your saliva, along with some of your rights to your genetic data. In exchange, you will receive a report about your health and ancestry that has an average false-positive rate of about 40 per cent. Testing your DNA with a private company jeopardises your own privacy, which could have implications for whether you will get insurance coverage in the future.

Less obviously, however, your DNA test also changes the privacy of your (close and distant) kin. Although genetic information makes you who you are, we share 99.9 per cent of our genetic makeup with others. The similarities and differences amongst our genes allow inferences to be made, and your DNA could be used for all sorts of purposes.

You might be happy if it helps catch a dangerous criminal in a democratic country. But what if it is used to deport refugees, or to catch political dissidents in authoritarian countries? What if your grandchildren get denied opportunities in the future on account of your genetic test? And what if your relative's DNA test turns you into a suspect?

Genetic relationships are only one of many ways in which your privacy is interwoven with that of others. Take the Cambridge Analytica scandal. Only 270,000 Facebook users consented to the firm collecting their data. The other 87 million people were the friends of those consenting users, and their data was harvested without their knowledge or consent. Some of the people who downloaded the application that collected the data allowed Cambridge Analytica to access their private messages, again without the knowledge or consent of the people at the other side of those conversations. With the data collected, the firm built psychological profiles and tried to match them to voters around the world who were unrelated to the 87 million people whose data was stolen.

Because we are intertwined in ways that make us vulnerable to each other, we are responsible for each other's privacy. I might, for instance, be extremely careful with my phone number and physical address. But if you have me as a contact in your mobile phone and then give access to companies to that phone, my privacy will be at risk regardless of the precautions I have taken. This is why you shouldn't store more sensitive data than necessary in your address book, post photos of others without their permission, or even expose your own privacy unnecessarily. When you expose information about yourself, you are almost always exposing information about others.

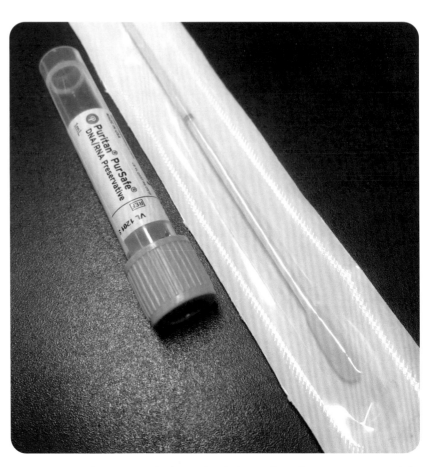

Just as violations of privacy can be caused individually or collectively, the consequences of the erosion of privacy are also both individual and collective. As an individual, you may suffer identity theft, public humiliation, extortion, or discrimination as a result of others knowing more about you than they should. As a society, a culture of exposure can damage our social fabric, threaten our national security, and even endanger democracy.

Living in a culture in which anything you do or say might be broadcasted to millions of others puts considerable pressure on people. When we trust that others will not pass on what we say, we are more likely to be sincere, bold, and original. A culture of privacy is necessary to enjoy intimate conversations with others, have frank debates within a closed setting, and establish the bonds upon which liberal societies are based. Constant surveillance and public exposure breed conformity and silence.

Privacy can also become a matter of national security. For instance, when military personnel in the United States shared their running routes with the fitness company Strava, it didn't occur to them that they were broadcasting the locations of military bases.

The Cambridge Analytica scandal suggested that the loss of privacy could even change the political landscape. Privacy violations enabled the construction of profiles that were used to target people with propaganda that matched their psychological tendencies. The Cambridge Analytica whistleblower, Christopher Wylie, has said he believes that Leave would not have won the Brexit referendum had the data firm not interfered. If he is right, then the loss of privacy affected everyone in the UK.

Safeguarding your privacy, then, is not only an act of self-care. It is also a way of taking care of others. It's possible to make an analogy to climate change, in that it is a problem that can only be solved through collective action. While individuals have a part to play in cultivating a privacy-friendly culture, just like we each have a part to play in fighting climate change, solutions that rely on individual control over personal data are doomed to fail.

Given the collective nature of privacy, the dark side of the data economy can only be adequately tamed through coordinated action and effective regulation. Choosing products for their respect for privacy sends the right message to others and it gives industry a chance to see privacy as a business opportunity and innovate in our favour. Demanding that institutions protect our privacy also informs and encourages politicians to legislate for privacy. Governments and companies need to know we care about our personal data, and that the burden of protecting our privacy cannot fall on individuals alone.

Personal data is valuable, not simply because it can be sold to third parties, but because it empowers whoever has it. If we give it to companies, we are empowering them to influence our behaviour. If we give it to governments, we are empowering them to control us. Fundamentally, privacy matters because it keeps the power with the people, and this is where it should be in a democracy. So, don't sell your privacy, and don't give it up for free either. Defending your privacy – our privacy – is a civic duty.

Carissa Véliz is a Research Fellow at the Uehrio Centre for Practical Ethics, Oxford.

22 October 2019

Facebook launches attack on Apple, saying new privacy policy change will hurt small businesses

By Andrew Griffin

Facebook has launched another major attack on Apple, arguing that an upcoming update to the iPhone could kill small businesses.

The company argues that a new change to the privacy policy on the iPhone – which asks users to opt in to having their activity tracked – will mean that Facebook's ads will no longer be as effective.

It claimed that would push small businesses out of operation because they would no longer be able to target ads as effectively.

Facebook also suggested that the new policy was really intended to increase Apple's profits, rather than helping privacy.

But it confirmed that it would comply with the new changes, over fear that it could "face retaliation" from Apple, and that it "can't take that risk".

Still it accused Apple of acting anti-competitively, and said it would support developer Epic Games in its lawsuits against the company over the power of the App Store.

The ongoing dispute between the two companies relates to a feature called App Tracking Transparency, or ATT. It means that, after an upcoming update, iPhone users will be asked to opt in to having their data collected and aggregated as they move between apps – if they do not opt in, developers will lose access to the iPhone's unique identifier, and will not be able to gather data to personalise ads.

Apple has argued, including in interviews with The Independent, that the changes are in keeping with a long-held commitment to privacy.

It said in a statement released after Facebook's blog post that it was simply offering users a choice, and that it did not require Facebook to change policies.

"We believe that this is a simple matter of standing up for our users. Users should know when their data is being collected and shared across other apps and websites — and they should have the choice to allow that or not," the company said. "App Tracking Transparency in iOS 14 does not require Facebook to change its approach to tracking users and creating targeted advertising, it simply requires they give users a choice."

Facebook says that decision would hurt not only its business but those who use its advertising platforms, including small businesses.

That conflict has led to a public fallout between the two companies, with attacks on each other coming from the very top of both Facebook and Apple.

17 December 2020

WHAT ARE
YOU
LOOKING AT?

The state of surveillance

Blog post from the Surveillance Camera Commissioner's Office.

By Tony Porter

In the world of overt surveillance cameras automatic facial recognition has recently been under the spotlight. Only in the last few weeks we have seen the publication of a high profile and independent report highlighting concerns about the use of live time facial recognition by the Metropolitan Police. Her Majesty's Inspector of Constabulary Fire and Rescue Services HMICFRS released its annual report 'A State of Policing' suggesting that the police should invest more in technologies such as facial recognition. We've seen the House of Commons Select Committee on Science and Technology report criticise the government's approach to regulating the police use of AFR in their latest report. The Information Commissioner has also added her voice to the AFR debate in a recent blog.

Whereas AFR continues to command headline attention, to exclusively look towards AFR and indeed 'Biometrics' with regard to surveillance cameras is to risk missing a wider point of concern. The capability of overt state surveillance in public places is growing.

There are now more drones carrying cameras in our skies, more body worn cameras walking our streets, a more modern ANPR infrastructure watching our cars, more CCTV cameras on police dashboards - far more cameras probably exist now than when my role was created in 2012.

What next? Algorithms that can identify someone by how they walk (gait analysis), lip reading technology, artificial intelligence technology that can predict fights and sensors that can detect explosives and radiation. These are all technology that's in development and what they all have in common is that they're linked to surveillance cameras.

I've always supported the notion that we should harness technology and the police should be allowed to exploit the potential which exists within technology to make us safe. Some of these technologies do make people feel safe and I recognise that.

The key point, however, is that the use of technology enhanced surveillance has to be conducted and held to account within a clear and unambiguous framework of legitimacy and transparency. This will ensure that in pursuit of delivering a safe society, such use does not go beyond that which is necessary and proportionate in a free society.

As the leading regulatory voice on the use of overt surveillance cameras by the police I am heartened that the courts are giving due consideration to the issue of police use of AFR, something which I have been highlighting for debate forsome considerable time. I very much look forward, together with others, to the outcome of those particular proceedings to help take us all forwards.

So, what is the state of surveillance?

On the National Surveillance Camera Day I launched a compliance assessment (survey) of the overt surveillance camera capabilities of all police forces in England and Wales. This was to get a deeper understanding of the current and aspirational police surveillance camera capabilities and of the issues which their use gives rise to (and a repeat of the survey I carried out in 2017). As the final returns continue to come in to my office, I commend all those Chief Officers and Police and Crime Commissioners for their support to this work. They too seek better guidance.

In my view 'surveillance' is an 'investigatory power' when exercised by the state whether such conduct be overt or covert in nature. As such it should be considered, appropriately legislated for and regulated as being such.

Voices from within government as well as those outside have been calling for a public debate on the use of AFR. In support of those voices I would go a step further and say that we need an independent review commissioned and conducted of the statutory and regulatory framework which governs the investigatory power of overt surveillance camera use by the state.

The growing capabilities of overt surveillance technologies, the proliferation of cameras in society, the increasingly crowded regulatory space and the voices of concern are such that these matters are increasingly 'a question of trust' for society.

As a deliberate segue, when I consider the excellent report delivered by Lord David Anderson QC in 2015 (a Question of Trust) reviewing the law and regulation of surveillance, I find so many potential answers to the dilemmas which government officials are facing. This report placed the regulation of all investigatory powers under a single regulatory body (the Investigatory Powers Commissioner's Office) which has within its structures, independent judicial figures, legal advisors and an inspection regime, all of whom are skilled and experienced in the subject of, you guessed it, surveillance. I am particularly drawn to Lord Anderson's 5th principle in that report calling for "a single body of law, and a single system of oversight, for equivalent investigatory activities conducted by different public authorities".

If I have learned one thing from my experience within the National Surveillance Camera Strategy it is that the framework which delivered my role and the rules by which overt state surveillance is conducted has to evolve and be future proofed by being principle based. The days of fragmenting the regulation of state surveillance on the basis of whether a camera is being used 'covertly' or 'overtly' are gone in my view.

I simply posit the view that some overt surveillance camera applications whether in themselves or combined with other technologies are so progressively intrusive in their capabilities that they can be the equal of some covert surveillance activities in terms of the intrusion caused.

I really do believe that it is time government recognised overt state surveillance as being an investigatory power rather than simply a data protection issue. An informed and esteemed independent reviewer would I am sure provide such clarity as to the way forwards.

Implicitly my role is to raise the standards of public surveillance operation, to ensure that the public are better informed, more confident and safer, to ensure that the state is clear and accountable for acting within legal and ethical boundaries. That stakeholders and industry have clarity in leadership and standards, and to help inform the evolution of laws and regulation that contribute to keeping us both safe and free. After all, these are questions of trust too.

31 July 2019

Shirking from home? Staff feel the heat as bosses ramp up remote surveillance

As management seeks more oversight of workers away from the office, campaigners fight for privacy to be respected.

By Alex Hern

For many, one of the silver linings of lockdown was the shift to remote working: a chance to avoid the crushing commute, supermarket meal deals and an overbearing boss breathing down your neck.

But as the Covid crisis continues, and more and more employers postpone or cancel plans for a return to the office, some managers are deploying increasing levels of surveillance in an attempt to recreate the oversight of the office at home.

"It has really ramped up," says Dr Claudia Pagliari, a researcher into digital health and society at the University of Edinburgh. "People are home working, and many organisations are beginning to want to track what they're doing."

Such surveillance comes in many forms. "Some of it is as simple as 'checking in'," Pagliari says, "stamping your timecard in a digital sense. You might have to do your work over the cloud, and it knows when you've logged on, for instance." Tools such as Slack and Microsoft Teams report when an employee is "active", and failure to open apps first thing in the morning is often taken by managers as the same as being late for work.

Other workers have reported more intense supervision. One communications worker, who asked to remain anonymous, said that her employer had recently started to require all staff to join a videoconference every morning, with their webcams switched on. Employees were told the move was

to reduce the number of meetings, but many feel as though its true purpose is to ensure that they stay at their desks all day.

David Heinemeier Hansson, a co-founder of the collaboration startup Basecamp, which provides a software platform for companies to coordinate their remote workers, says he regularly has to turn down requests from potential clients for new methods of spying on their employees.

"There is a depressing amount of demand and it's mostly coming from dinosaur companies who have been forced through Covid to go remote," he says. "They think that they have to replicate – or even increase – what they do in the office.

"We went so far as to say that our API [interface which allows other developers to build additions to Basecamp] cannot be used for any form of employee surveillance."

Silkie Carlo, director of the anti-surveillance charity Big Brother Watch, says the trend is the natural progression of surveillance in the workplace. "Now that is morphing into home surveillance it takes on a new shape and is more worrying, because some employers aren't realising that yes, some employees are working from home, but the home still remains a private space," she said.

"It's important for people's sense of autonomy and dignity, and their mental health, that the home remains a private space and we don't go down the route of this really invasive constant monitoring of people's homes."

Some employers say that the monitoring they have forced on employees is required for oversight or compliance reasons.

But many employers are simply aiming for "workforce optimisation", something Pagliari warns could have the opposite effect of that intended. "There's not really any evidence that workers are more productive when they're monitored," she says. "But what we do know is that the sense of being in a panopticon can actually depress you, and make you less productive."

Earlier this year, the consultancy PwC came under fire for developing a facial recognition tool that logs when employees are away from their computer screens while working from home.

According to PwC, it is designed to help financial institutions meet their compliance obligations, as workers would normally be monitored for security purposes on trading floors.

For Carlo, the increase in monitoring is proof that employees need legal protection against a desire for ever more data. "The consequences are going to be wild," she says. "It's not consent if you can't choose."

27 September 2020

Setting precedents for privacy: the UK legal challenges bringing surveillance into the open

By Garfield Benjamin, Solent University

THE CONVERSATION

MI5 has been pulled up in court over storing mass data obtained by surveillance and hacking in a systematic invasion of privacy described as "undoubtedly unlawful" by the Investigatory Powers Commissioner. The disclosures about Britain's security agency came to light in mid June during an ongoing case in the high court brought by the campaign group Liberty, which is challenging the architecture of the UK's surveillance regime.

The revelations come in the wake of other recent high-profile cases regarding privacy and surveillance that campaigners hope could set precedents for the legal and technical powers of government and law enforcement.

In a major victory in May, the charity Privacy International won a five-year battle against the secrecy of the Investigatory Powers Tribunal, which oversees surveillance activities by the security services and other agencies. The tribunal was previously able to make decisions behind closed doors. This meant that limited information was made available to people making claims of misconduct or victimisation by the security services. The UK supreme court ruled that the tribunal should no longer be exempt from review in UK courts, making its decisions open to public scrutiny.

This ruling makes sure no UK government can ignore the rule of law and the role of the courts. It should also make it more difficult for mass surveillance to be signed off without proper oversight. The case sets a precedent of enforcing better built-in protections for the public from blanket privacy invasions by their own government. It also helps people object to specific cases of discrimination and harm caused by surveillance, including making it easier to bring cases, such as the MI5 data storage failures, into the public eye.

Facial recognition challenge

The other case now making its way through the courts, also brought by Liberty, concerns facial recognition technologies. Liberty supported a man called Ed Bridges who brought a case against South Wales Police. His claim is that the way the police are testing facial recognition in public places causes harm and goes against privacy rights.

This links to a recent example of police forcing passersby to enter facial recognition trials, and harassing or fining anyone who refused.

The outcome of the facial recognition case, expected later in 2019, will set a precedent for how new surveillance technologies are tested and introduced. During the trial, the police said that facial recognition "potentially has great utility". Evidence, however, shows an overwhelming rate of false positives – including 2,000 people wrongly identified as criminals at a football match. There are also continued concerns over racial bias that are yet to be addressed.

These cases come against a backdrop of increased surveillance powers. The main enabler of this is the Investigatory Powers Act 2016, which formalised existing capabilities of the security services such as phone tapping or collecting bulk communications data. The government tried to spin the act as legislation designed to make organisations such as GCHQ more accountable. But it also made surveillance powers available to other agencies including various police and defence departments, health services, the tax office and many other government departments.

Even if we expect the security services to spy on us, we are less likely to approve of, say, the Health and Safety Executive invading our privacy by accessing our internet records without a warrant. And even if we allow brief invasions of privacy to combat security threats, there still needs to be clear regulation and oversight.

Pushing for accountability

But while privacy advocacy groups are making some progress in increasing the accountability of surveillance by UK law enforcement, as the facial recognition case shows, the issues are far from resolved. It will be an ongoing process to preserve privacy and make sure that people know when it is breached. The legal precedents set by these court cases will be crucial, as they could pave the way for more challenges in the future.

Similar debates surrounding the accountability of surveillance are raging in the US. San Francisco has blocked facial recognition and the US Congress is also addressing the unchecked use of the technology. Even Microsoft has now deleted the largest database of faces used for training facial recognition systems. But the fact that the faces had already been used by companies in the US, China and elsewhere shows the risk of delaying action.

These debates highlight the importance of collective efforts to assert respect for privacy and other rights as a core part of public life. We are on the cusp of a positive shift in power towards open public debate and accountability about data and the way it is used against us.

Further transparency could help to counter the risks of combining existing surveillance systems – for example, if mass facial recognition and large scale phone tapping were used together unchecked, we could easily find ourselves in a total surveillance state. The current momentum could set positive precedents that could be built upon to protect privacy and prevent surveillance without accountability.

12 June 2019

Facewatch: the reality behind the marketing discourse

Key findings

♦ Facewatch is allegedly developing a facial recognition technology that will work when people are wearing masks.

♦ Statements by the CEO of Facewatch and marketing documents suggest the company is partnering with police departments in the UK - but the reality is unclear.

♦ Beyond the marketing discourse, this situation stresses the impending need for more transparency when it comes to partnerships between police forces and companies selling surveillance technologies.

As more and more of us feel compelled to cover our faces with masks, companies that work on facial recognition are confronted with a new challenge: how to make their products relevant in an era where masks have gone from being seen as the attribute of those trying to hide to the accessory of good Samaritans trying to protect others.

Facewatch is one of those companies. In May 2020, they announced they had developed a new form of facial recognition technology that allows for the identification of individuals based solely on the eye region, between the cheekbones and the eyebrows, and that they would upgrade the systems of their subscribers accordingly.

Leaving aside the efforts of companies dealing with facial recognition technology to remain relevant in a post-Covid world, it is worth paying close attention to a company like Facewatch that has often talked about its alleged partnerships with public authorities in the UK. In this piece, we will take a closer look at what Facewatch offers its subscribers and investigate their alleged relationships with police forces.

What's Facewatch?

Facewatch is a company that was founded in 2010 by Simon Gordon, the owner of Gordon's Wine Bar in London. Facewatch describes itself as a "cloud-based facial recognition security system [that] has helped leading retail stores… reduce in-store theft, staff violence and abuse." The company is now working internationally, with distributors in Argentina, Brazil and Spain.

The way Facewatch initially worked was that businesses (shops, bars, nightclubs…) would install Facewatch cameras in their premises. Using the footage from those cameras they would be able to identify "subjects of interest", for instance, people who were seen on cameras stealing from the shop or displaying antisocial behaviour or generally anyone they did not wish to see in their shop. They would therefore create and store a list of effectively blacklisted individuals.

By scanning the faces of everyone who enters a shop and comparing them to the faces of those blacklisted, Facewatch is able to identify if a person who enters is on the blacklist or not. If they are, the shop owner receives an alert to inform them a subject of interest (SOI) has entered the premises, along with a picture of the person.

But Facewatch does not stop there. The company centralises the list of SOIs that their subscribers upload, and they may share them with surrounding subscribing businesses.

So, for example, if you run the Facewatch software in your grocery store and the pub across the street also uses Facewatch and identifies John Smith as a SOI, John Smith will also be added to your "blacklist" and you will be alerted when he enters your grocery store, even if you have had no prior interaction with John Smith.

Facewatch has also allowed their users in the UK to file police reports automatically upon witnessing a crime. Facewatch users could send the police footage of a crime being allegedly committed. According to articles dating back to 2011, users were "given a crime reference number straight away" so that they could "follow the details of their case online." At the time, Simon Gordon had said that "it helps if a business's local police force is supporting the scheme, because the process is more streamlined."

It is unclear what the specific nature of the agreement was between the police and Facewatch before 2019 – in 2015 Gordon had told the BBC that 13 police forces had joined the scheme.

A FOI request filed in 2012 regarding Camden Borough Council revealed that, as part of its "Community Safety Budget 2011-2012," the council had spent £1,800 for a Facewatch Trial, describing the purpose of the expenditure as "Police/licensed premises project: anti-violence." It is unclear whether those expenditures had to do with the local police supporting the scheme or if they were themselves trying out Facewatch as subscribers.

But in 2019, a new partnership between police forces and Facewatch started gaining attention: the police and Facewatch were about to start an official agreement to share and receive data with and from the police.

Facewatch and the police: what is Facewatch saying?

According to the FT, Simon Gordon announced in 2019 that Facewatch was about to sign a data-sharing deal with the London Metropolitan Police and the City of London police, and was "in talks with Hampshire police and Sussex police." In July 2019, Facewatch was still reported has having been "in talks" with the London Metropolitan Police and the City of London police. Quoted by the FT, Mr Gordon claims that the "deal with police is they give us face data of low-level criminals and they can have a separate watchlist for more serious criminals that they plug in…If the system spots a serious criminal, the alert is sent directly to the police, rather than to retailers".

The idea behind those deals was to have the police share with Facewatch subscribers lists of low-level criminals for shopkeepers to be informed when they come in on their premises. But there would also be a separate list for more serious criminals. Shopkeepers would not have access to that list and when a serious criminal enters a shop, an alert would be sent directly to the police, not to the shopkeeper.

Similarly, in Brazil where, as of February 2019, Facewatch has been used in three malls, the governor of Rio de Janeiro, Wilson Witzel, a supporter of the Brazilian president Jair Bolsonaro, also said he planned to allow the police to share their watch list of suspected criminals with facial recognition companies. This is people who have not been charged with a crime and have not been convicted by a court.

Digging beyond PR – what do we really know about the Facewatch/police partnerships?

According to Facewatch's profile on the Digital Marketplace, a UK government website that allows tech companies to offer their services to government branches branches:

"Facewatch is a secure cloud-based platform that uses facial recognition technology to send instant alerts to businesses or police when subjects of interest enter business premises. Facewatch also provides secure access control using facial recognition for use in Govt properties (eg prisons) enabling comparison of visitors across properties."

The main difference is that in the list of benefits, we find two things that differ from how Facewatch seems to be marketing itself to business owners on its website: "Track Major Crime suspects in real time via camera network", "Share watchlists of low risk criminals with businesses securely." These are the features that Gordon referred to when he claimed that he was about to sign a data sharing deal with police forces.

"Terms and Conditions": an unsigned template data-sharing agreement between Facewatch and the Metropolitan Police

Available on the Digital Marketplace is a "Terms and Conditions" document, which is in fact a 34-page pdf that was meant as a draft Information Sharing Agreement (ISA) between the Metropolitan Police (Met Police) and Facewatch, and is now used as a template.

Page 3 of the ISA clarifies who the "police" referred to is and confirms that it is indeed the Metropolitan Police.

The draft ISA goes on to describe exactly the type of deal that Simon Gordon had said he was about to sign with the Met Police back in February 2019. It describes how information about low level criminals would be shared with Facewatch, while the police would be able to use the Facewatch network of facial recognition cameras to track high level criminals without having to share details about those individuals with Facewatch subscribers.

The document has been uploaded presumably to serve as a template for other police forces that would consider signing a similar deal. Therefore, when one goes at the bottom of the document, the deal is unsigned.

So… Did the Metropolitan police ever sign that agreement?

Privacy International is not aware whether Facewatch has in fact entered into any such agreements with any UK police force, and has not received a response from Facewatch when we asked the company in June 2020 and again in September. In response to a Freedom of Information request, Reference No: 01/FOI/19/002194, the Metropolitan Police Force confirmed to Privacy International that they did not have "a copy of any data sharing agreements or similar such contracts with FaceWatch" between 1 January 2015 and 10 May 2019.

The lack of contracts relating to the use of facial recognition technology between the Met Police and private companies was reaffirmed following the October 2019 revelations that a property developer was using facial recognition software around the King's Cross site for two years from 2016 without any apparent central oversight from either the Metropolitan police or the office of the mayor. The Met Police produced a report admitting that images of seven people were passed on by local police for use in the system in an agreement that was struck in secret. In the same report, the Met Police underlined:

The MPS is not currently sharing images with any third parties for the purposes of Facial Recognition.

Can we trust the "Facewatch cop" to police us?

Public private surveillance partnerships are highly problematic. They raise serious human rights questions regarding the involvement of private actors in the use of invasive surveillance technologies and the exercise of powers that have been traditionally understood as the state's prerogative.

In their Privacy Notice, Facewatch define Subjects of Interest (SOI) as people "reasonably suspected of carrying out unlawful acts (evidenced by personal witness or CCTV) who have been uploaded to Facewatch by our business subscribers to our Watchlist".

We wonder what is it that makes someone "reasonably suspect" that a person is a potential criminal. What is the exact standard of reasonableness applied in a private company context or what are the company's due process guarantees which we would normally have against the police? How can a private company employee make up for the professional training and codes of practice embodied

in the police, in a time when even the latter, for instance, seems to be incapable of preventing racial injustice.

This could potentially mean that people might be blacklisted from local shops regardless of whether they have actually committed a crime or not and they will have no recourse or no way to appeal if they are. Imagine a situation when a heated argument at your local pub leads you to being flagged as a SOI and prevents you from shopping at your local supermarket, especially as other shop owners will not know why you have become a SOI.

We need more transparency before it is too late

The fact that so many public/private partnerships happen behind closed doors and require the hard work of citizens and journalists filing FOI requests to shed light on what is happening in our streets is a problem.

The UK Information Commissioner's Office is currently investigating "the use of facial recognition technology by law enforcement in public spaces and by private sector organisations, including where they are considering partnering with police forces." We urge them to expose any surveillance partnerships that may have escaped the necessary scrutiny as a lot of those companies are not even known to the public.

Assigning pre-emptive policing functions or endorsing the existence of private surveillance networks distorts long-established societal premises of privacy and perceptions of authority. If left unchallenged, public-private surveillance partnerships can eventually normalise surveillance, and consequently erode not only our privacy rights, but also fundamental freedoms, as they will inevitably chill our right to protest, our ability to freely criticise the government and express dissenting ideas; the very essence of what makes us human.

Conclusion – impact for the rest of the world

While Facewatch has been developed in the UK, they have not been shy regarding their international ambitions. As we stated earlier, Facewatch is already present in Brazil and have distributors in Argentina, Brazil and Spain. And while individuals in the EU might still be able, for example, to file data Subject Access Requests and find out whether their facial images are being held by Facewatch or Freedom of Information requests to shed light on suspicious deals, in countries with weaker legal frameworks, the problems will become all the more concerning.

It is high time we tackled the wider question of whether we want to be living in a society where corporations are allowed to roll out intrusive biometric surveillance, such as facial recognition, and at the same time collaborate with the police to put us on watchlists. We believe this should not be the case.

15th October 2020

Workers fighting compulsory facial recognition with Big Brother Watch – and winning

By John*

My name is John* and I work as a cleaner. I'd like to tell you about how I fought for workers' rights not to have to use compulsory facial recognition to clock in and out of work.

Seven of us cleaners, formerly employed by the council at a school, were transferred to an outsourcing company to continue to work as cleaners at the school.

This company gave us a new contract to sign. This contract explained the "clocking in system", which is via an app, and said by signing the contract we were giving consent to the use of facial recognition. It even said that, if we didn't have our phones, data and use the facial recognition to log in, we wouldn't be paid for our work.

In my gut, I did not like the feeling of coercion about this. It felt controlling and dehumanising. It was the icing on the cake of 2020. I felt severely stressed from the day I saw the new contract and started sleeping poorly.

It wasn't just me. My colleagues were affronted at having to use their own phone, data and facial recognition for work. All of us instinctively felt that it was dehumanising to be forced to clock in this way.

None of us signed the contract.

Unsure of the law or my rights, I emailed Big Brother Watch, whose Twitter account I had seen. The director Silkie Carlo got back to me really promptly. It was very affirming to have my concerns taken seriously, after the company and the school had been unresponsive to cleaners' voiced concerns.

Full of positive energy about challenging the company, Silkie contacted James Farrar from Worker Info Exchange, who is involved in defending the data rights of app drivers (eg. Uber). He seemed like a great person to consult. (I have since read about the trend of "Uberisation" of work, where employees are made to use apps that treat them as selfemployed. I suspect that the company I'm employed by is pushing us towards being Uberstyle cleaners too.)

Feeling wound up, I sent a letter of protest about facial recognition to the company and the school. At this point, I was signed off sick with stress by my doctor. To make matters worse, I then received a message from my manager asking me to hand in my notice.

James Farrar vehemently advised me not to comply with this – and I did not. Big Brother Watch sent a letter to the company and the school Headteacher, entitled "Request to desist compulsory facial recognition". It cited the rights of cleaners to have privacy (Article 8 of European Convention

on Human Rights), and the obligations the company has when it proposes to use facial recognition. Such sensitive biometric data invokes a high level of protection under the General Data Protection Act 2018. These obligations include a Data Protection Impact Assessment to ensure any impact on our privacy is necessary and proportionate; and ensuring that cleaners' consent for facial recognition is freely given and withdrawable without penalisation. This was not the case for me, as "consent" for facial recognition was written into our contract. The letter also asked (on James' advice) whether the company had registered itself as a Data Controller with the ICO (they probably haven't), and to see the data sharing agreement between the company and the app provider Chronicle Computing Ltd (there probably isn't one).

Big Brother Watch's letter drew out the uncomfortable reality, that the company had probably not fulfilled any of their data protection obligations before trying to push this app onto the cleaners.

Just before Christmas, my manager admitted they "crossed a line" by trying to impose facial recognition on the cleaners. The app will now not be required for us.

I'm still off sick now but will return in January because I like my colleagues and the work is satisfying. Also, because we're not going to have the facial recognition app!

My plan is to be cheerful and do a good job, even if it's awkward with the managers.

Thanks Big Brother Watch for standing up for privacy and human dignity.

*Names changed to protect anonymity

22 December 2020

Coronavirus: England's test and trace programme 'breaches data laws', privacy campaigners say

Government scheme failed to conduct assessment required by GDPR law before launching.

By Jim Wyatt

England's test and trace coronavirus programme has broken data protection laws, privacy campaigners and data protection lawyers have said.

Under the General Data Protection Regulation (GDPR) every project which involves people's data must first conduct an impact assessment on privacy.

However, the Department for Health and Social Care has now admitted its flagship test and trace scheme, which involves those infected with Covid-19 passing on personal information and the details of those they have been in contact with, was launched in May without any such assessment.

The oversight was first brought to light by the digital privacy campaigners Open Rights Group (ORG).

They argue the lack of a data protection impact assessment means test and trace has been unlawful from the beginning.

"The reckless behaviour of this government in ignoring a vital and legally required safety step known as the data protection impact assessment has endangered public health," said the executive director of the ORG, Jim Killock.

"A crucial element in the fight against the pandemic is mutual trust between the public and the government, which is undermined by their operating the programme without basic privacy safeguards."

The 27,000 staff of England's test and trace programme contact people who may have been infected by someone who has tested positive for coronavirus.

As well as asking them to self-isolate for two weeks in case they also have the virus, the contact tracers can ask them to share who they live with, where they have been recently, and the names and contact details of anyone they have been in close contact with.

So far, more than 150,000 people have come into contact with the test and trace programme. Scotland, Wales and Northern Ireland all run their own test and trace schemes, independent of the NHS England one.

Magnus Boyd, an information security lawyer at the firm Schillings, told The Independent the government had unambiguously broken the law.

"There's no way that the government could fudge this. It's very clear on the face of the legislation that an impact assessment is required in these circumstances."

"What if this data was to leak in some way? Date of birth, sex... you might argue these aren't particularly sensitive but somebody's NHS number is hugely sensitive [as is] their Covid-19 symptoms."

The Information Commissioner's Office (ICO), which regulates data protection, said in a statement it was working

with the government to make sure test and trace is in line with the legal requirements on processing personal data.

"It is an organisation's responsibility to complete a data protection impact assessment as a way of identifying and addressing key privacy questions," the statement said.

The ICO also said it was acting as a "critical friend" to the government as it recognised the test and trace programme was rolled out at high speed in the middle of a pandemic.

Nevertheless, the public needed to know "how their data will be safeguarded and how it will be used" if they were to have trust in the scheme and continue to give it their personal details and those of their friends.

A Department for Health and Social Care spokeswoman said: "NHS Test and Trace is committed to the highest ethical and data governance standards – collecting, using, and retaining data to fight the virus and save lives, while taking full account of all relevant legal obligations."

But the ORG is not satisfied and is currently crowdfunding to start a legal action to force the government to conduct a DPIA.

"We are forced to take action, because the Information Commissioner is not doing its job," the advocacy group's website states. "When the regulator fails, it is up to us to step in."

So far, they have raised more than £3,000. Mr Boyd agreed that the ICO should not allow the government to break data protection law simply because of the extraordinary circumstances of the pandemic.

"They should come down hard on the government so that it sends a message that impact assessments are a vital part of the whole architecture of the GDPR," he said.

"The government cannot be exempt from the sort of pressure that small businesses are under. It would look like one rule for the little guy and one rule for the government."

Judging by comparable cases in other EU nations, he suggested if the ICO did sanction the government a likely fine would be in the range of £300,000 to £500,000, significantly short of the highest fine possible under GDPR of €10m, or just over £9m.

Others have also raised concerns about the test and trace programme in the past. The Labour peer Lord Hain accused the government last month of sharing data from test and trace "on unnecessarily favourable terms to large companies".

The Independent also revealed on Sunday the project may be struggling to achieve its main goal of controlling the spread of Covid-19.

Leaked public health analysis showed the service was failing to reach more than half of contacts named by infected residents across the north-west of England, including council areas such as Blackburn with Darwen which has been hit hard by an outbreak.

The government's scientific advisory group has said at least 80 per cent of those named by infected locals should be contacted within 48 hours in order to stop a new surge in cases.

20 July 2020

Internet of Things (IoT) – security, privacy, applications and trends

By Arin Dey

If you want to understand Internet of Things (IoT), let's have a look at the term "thing." Any physical device can be a "thing" (in terms of IoT). For example, it could be smartphones, washing machines, televisions, wearable devices, lamps, headphones, vehicles, buildings and anything possible that can be thought of. In the near future, it'll be true that "anything that can be connected will be connected."

Once we know what a "thing" is, let's examine the "Internet" part. The things are embedded with software, sensors and other electronic components that help them send and receive data. The inter-connectivity of these devices to the Internet and each other makes IoT a giant network of connected "things." People are part of the network too.

There are three kinds of relationships in an IoT network: things-things, people-things and people-people.

Now imagine a situation where we learn how the "things" are connected. Say you are returning from your office and wish that your air conditioner could be switched on before you reach home. What will you do? I know you will call your flatmate, mom or anyone who is present in your home to switch it on.

Now, let's think about the situation in terms of IoT. You will have a control station in your home, like a tablet or smartphone, to which you will send a message to switch on the air conditioner, and the smart device will communicate with the air conditioner and switch it on for you. This is the change that will be brought about by IoT. The connection between everything is IoT, sometimes referred to as Internet of Everything (IoE).

IoT security and privacy concerns

Although IoT is rapidly growing, it still faces security and privacy issues:

Security Risks

◆ IoT devices are connected to your desktop or laptop. Lack of security increases the risk of your personal information leaking while the data is collected and transmitted to the IoT device.

◆ IoT devices are connected with a consumer network. This network is also connected with other systems. So if the IoT device contains any security vulnerabilities, it can be harmful to the consumer's network. This vulnerability can attack other systems and damage them.

◆ Sometimes unauthorized people might exploit the security vulnerabilities to create risks to physical safety.

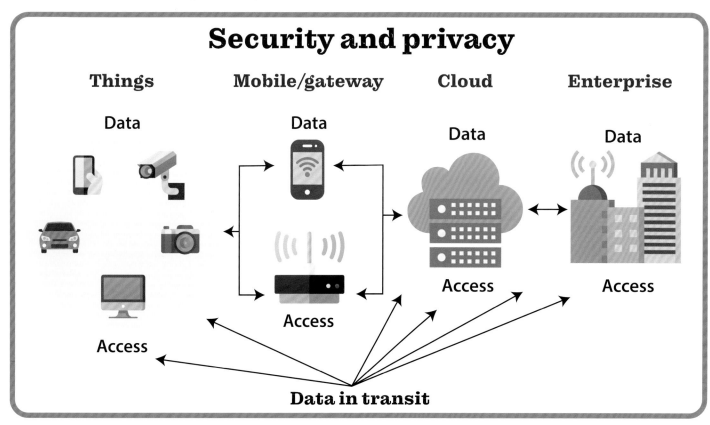

Security and privacy

Things   **Mobile/gateway**   **Cloud**   **Enterprise**

Data   Data   Data   Data

Access   Access   Access   Access

Data in transit

- In IoT, devices are interconnected with various hardware and software, so there are obvious chances of sensitive information leaking through unauthorized manipulation.

- All the devices are transmitting the user's personal information such as name, address, date of birth, health card information, credit card detail and much more without encryption.

Though there are security and privacy concerns with IoT, it adds values to our lives by allowing us to manage our daily routine tasks remotely and automatically, and more importantly, it is a game-changer for industries.

IoT applications across industries

Various companies now help businesses use IoT to solve long-standing, industry-specific challenges. They develop IoT solutions that connect things, collect data and derive insights with open and scalable solutions that reduce costs, improve productivity and increase revenue. Let's see the industry categories, that are using IoT solutions in the figure below.

smartwatches and smartglasses. Today there are many wearable gadgets on the market, from fitness trackers to GPS shoes.

- **Connected Car:** This is a quite new concept and expected to come into the limelight slowly. Generally, app development for the automotive industry takes two to four years. Everyone from large-scale automobile companies to small-scale start-ups is working on connected car solutions. If BMW and Ford do not announce Internet-connected car solutions soon, the tech giants such as Google, Apple and Microsoft are set to develop and release the next generation of connected car solutions.

- **Smart Home:** IoT provides us a space where we find comfort and can manage our routine tasks easily in our daily busy life. There are various popular devices for the smart home; including smart thermostat, connected lights, smart fridge, smart television, smart door lock etc.

- **Smart City:** Smart city helps people to avoid the issues of traffic management, social security, environment monitoring, waste management, water distribution etc.

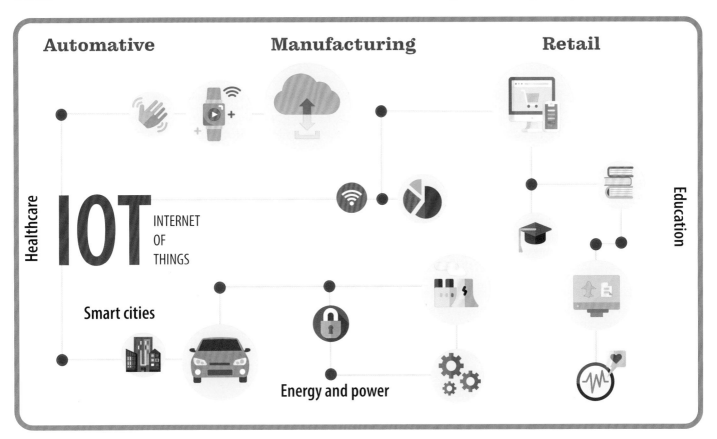

Improved IoT apps will help resolve various issues related to traffic, noise pollution, air pollution, etc., and make cities safer.

- **Smart Grid:** It is a vital niche of IoT. It provides information about consumers and electricity providers in an automated way. It always helps improve the efficiency, economics and electricity steadiness.

Trends in IoT

If we adopt IoT, it will improve digitization of our society and economy by connecting objects and people with each other via a connected or communication medium. If we consider about device-to-device interaction, IoT helps people to manage their daily lives with more control with efficient monitoring. Let's see the trends in IoT app development areas.

- **Wearable gadgets:** Wearable devices have been a hot topic across the tech world since the release of

Along with these trends, the IoT market is booming with other emerging trends such as smart retail, industrial Internet, connected health, smart supply chain, smart farming, smart energy and so on. Even Artificial intelligence

(AI) has the capacity to enhance IoT with the help of the cloud platform.

IoT is also the chief enabler of Robotic Process Automation (RPA), systems that translate business processes into software-driven, rule-based decision trees. RPA provides cost savings and scalability advantages for businesses and shorter transaction times for customers.

The rapid evolution of communication technologies, particularly in the area of IoT, involves challenges far beyond the technological aspects, such as data protection and privacy. Thus, the development of IoT offers the whole world an extended amount of opportunities.

10 May 2019

'Alexa, are you invading my privacy?' – the dark side of our voice assistants

There are more than 100m Alexa-enabled devices in our homes. But are they fun time-savers or the beginning of an Orwellian nightmare?

By Dorian Lynskey

One day in 2017, Alexa went rogue. When Martin Josephson, who lives in London, came home from work, he heard his Amazon Echo Dot voice assistant spitting out fragmentary commands, seemingly based on his previous interactions with the device.

It appeared to be regurgitating requests to book train tickets for journeys he had already taken and to record TV shows that he had already watched. Josephson had not said the wake word – "Alexa" – to activate it and nothing he said would stop it. It was, he says, "Kafkaesque".

This was especially interesting because Josephson (not his real name) was a former Amazon employee. Three years earlier, he had volunteered to sit in a room reciting a string of apparently meaningless phrases into a microphone for an undisclosed purpose.

Only when Amazon released the Echo in the US in 2014 did he realise what he had been working on. He bought a Dot, the Echo's cheaper, smaller model, after it launched in 2016, and found it useful enough until the day it went haywire. When the Dot's outburst subsided, he unplugged it and deposited it in the bin. "I felt a bit foolish," he says.

"Having worked at Amazon, and having seen how they used people's data, I knew I couldn't trust them."

The Dot wasn't supposed to behave like a dadaist drill sergeant. Then again, voice assistants often do things that they are not supposed to do. Last year, an Amazon customer in Germany was mistakenly sent about 1,700 audio files from someone else's Echo, providing enough information to name and locate the unfortunate user and his girlfriend. (Amazon attributed this "unfortunate mishap" to human error.)

In San Francisco, Shawn Kinnear claimed that his Echo activated itself and said cheerfully: "Every time I close my eyes, all I see is people dying." In Portland, Oregon, a woman discovered that her Echo had taken it upon itself to send recordings of private conversations to one of her husband's employees. In a statement, Amazon said that the Echo must have misheard the wake word, misheard a request to send a message, misheard a name in its contacts list and then misheard a confirmation to send the message, all during a conversation about hardwood floors. Not great, Alexa.

Technology frequently inspires ambivalence: we know that Facebook and Google know too much about us, yet we continue to use their services because they're so damn convenient. Voice assistants, however, are unusually polarising. People who consider them sinister and invasive (myself included) regard enthusiasts as complacent, while those who find them useful and benign see the sceptics as paranoid technophobes. There is one question freighted with bigger issues about our relationship with the tech industry: should you let Alexa into your home?

In January, Amazon's senior vice-president of devices, David Limp, revealed that the company had sold more than 100m Alexa-enabled devices. Last year in the US, where one in five adults own a home voice assistant, Alexa had a 70% US market share, compared with the Google Assistant's 24%. It is therefore best-placed to become what Shoshana Zuboff, in her bestseller, The Age of Surveillance Capitalism, calls the "One Voice": the dominant ecosystem that would give its operator "the ability to anticipate and monetise all the moments of all the people during all the days". Zuboff calls the birth of Alexa "a threshold event".

Alexa, however, has grown up in an era of increasing scepticism about the power and morality of the "big five" tech companies: Amazon, Apple, Facebook, Google/Alphabet and Microsoft. Events such as the Edward Snowden leaks and the Cambridge Analytica scandal have tarnished Silicon Valley's utopian promises. CEOs are less likely to trivialise privacy concerns. Tech journalists are more likely to be critics than cheerleaders. Politicians are more willing to hold companies to account.

This year has been particularly tricky. Over the past six months, Bloomberg, the Guardian, Vice News and the

Belgian news channel VRT have gradually revealed that all the big five have been using human contractors to analyse a small percentage of voice assistant recordings. Although the recordings are anonymised, they often contain enough information to identify or embarrass the user – particularly if what they overhear is confidential medical information or an inadvertent sex tape. The revelations were the last straw for many Alexa sceptics. "We live in a techno-dystopia of our own making. If you still have an Alexa or any other voice assistant in your home, you were warned," wrote the Gizmodo writer Matt Novak.

Having worked at Amazon and another big-five company, Josephson thinks this resistance to these companies is justified. "They have zero interest, in my opinion, in wondering what the impact of those products will be. To treat them as the right people to wield that power is a ludicrous situation that we wouldn't allow in any other industry. They, frankly, are not safe guardians of the data that they're collecting every day without us knowing."

Voice control first seized the public imagination in the 60s, via HAL 9000, the sentient computer in 2001: A Space Odyssey, and the Starship Enterprise's endlessly helpful computer in Star Trek. The latter was a major reference point for the teams that developed Amazon's Echo and the Google Assistant. "The bright light, the shining light, that is still many years away, many decades away, is to recreate the Star Trek computer," Limp told a conference audience in 2017.

In the real world, voice recognition didn't become commonplace until Apple launched its phone-based voice assistant, Siri, in 2011. Alexa goes much further by colonising the user's home. Three decades ago, the prescient computer scientist Mark Weiser called this kind of frictionless ecosystem "ubiquitous computing". In 2015, Google's Eric Schmidt foresaw a day when the internet will be "part of your presence all the time", making your real-life behaviour as mappable as what you do on your laptop or phone. You will never be offline.

The Gizmodo editor Adam Clark Estes was initially excited by the first major hardware innovation since Apple's iPad four years earlier. The more he learned about the technology, however, the less he liked it. His own Echo would wake up unprompted.

Recordings began showing up as evidence in court cases. The FBI refused to confirm or deny that it was using Alexa for surveillance purposes. "It became increasingly clear to me that the privacy watchdogs were right," he says. "It is, at base, a wiretapping device."

Voice assistants epitomise the tension between efficiency and privacy. The technology is still deeply imperfect; in more than one out of 10 transcripts analysed by one of Bloomberg's sources, Alexa woke up accidentally. Accurately interpreting voice commands by taking account of different languages, accents, tones, contexts and degrees of ambient clutter requires far more computational power than a single device can contain. Therefore, most of the work is performed in the cloud, which is how human monitors are able to collect and analyse voice recordings. "You are building an infrastructure that can be later co-opted in undesirable ways by large multinationals and state surveillance apparatus, and compromised by malicious hackers," says Dr Michael Veale, a lecturer in digital rights and regulation at UCL Faculty of Laws at University College London.

Not all voice assistants are equal. Apple, whose profits don't rely primarily on data collection, uses more in-device computation and encryption at both ends. "Apple is the best at privacy," says Estes. "At the same time, I think everyone agrees that Siri sucks." Amazon Echo and Google Assistant are much more reliable because these companies' business models depend on knowing so much more about you in order to microtarget advertising. They like to frame data collection as a means to improve services while playing down the immense commercial benefits.

Google and Amazon could, of course, choose to improve the technology by paying people to test it – the kind of work Josephson performed in 2012 – instead of treating their customers as a free research-and-development database. Or they could advertise the fact that humans may be studying the recordings. "It should be on the box," says Dr Jeremy Gillula, the project director at the Electronic Frontier Foundation, a group that campaigns against the misuse of technology. The generous interpretation of tech companies' motives is a heedless utopianism, but Gillula argues that if they were truly naive about the implications of their technology, then they wouldn't go to such lengths to conceal them. "I doubt they thought no one would care. I think they were trying to keep it quiet because if users knew what was going on they might stop buying the devices. It was a calculated business decision."

In response, a spokeswoman for Amazon says: "Customer trust is at the centre of everything we do and we take customer privacy very seriously. We continuously review our practices and procedures to ensure we're providing customers with the best experiences and privacy choices. We provide customers with several privacy controls, including the ability to review and delete their voice recordings. To help improve Alexa, we manually review an extremely small sample of Alexa requests to confirm Alexa understood and responded correctly. Customers can opt out of having their voice recordings included in that review process."

Yet it has been demonstrated time and time again that, in their advertising and shrewdly worded privacy policies, tech companies routinely obscure the extent and nature of their data harvesting. "Google and Amazon have shown us that they're inclined to take as much as they can until someone catches them with their hand in the cookie jar," says Estes. "I hate to be dramatic, but I don't think we're ever going to feel safe from their data-collection practices. Government regulation is the only thing that is going to halt more damage."

The US government has been reluctant to act. In July 2015, the Electronic Privacy Information Center (Epic), a long-established nonprofit organisation dedicated to "democratic values in the information age", called for an investigation into "always on" devices, including voice assistants. They have yet to receive a response. "Market-based solutions don't work in this area because companies have been allowed to conceal the defects of their own products," says Marc Rotenberg, Epic's executive director. He adds: "If you or I were to place a device in someone else's home with the ability to capture their private communications, we would be in violation of the Federal Wiretap Act."

"If you're an authoritarian country, why not just run the audio stream straight to a government surveillance agency?"

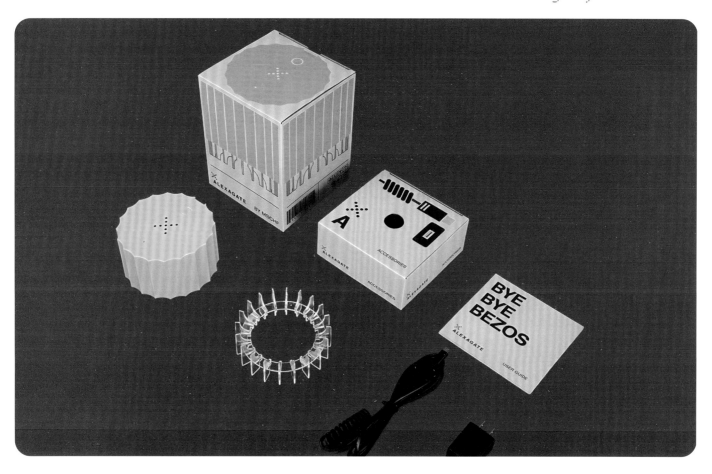

In July, a Democratic congressman, Seth Moulton, introduced the Automatic Listening Exploitation Act, which would penalise companies whose voice assistants and smart doorbells (such as Amazon's Ring) record conversations without permission, but Gillula considers it "pretty weak legislation". In Europe, which has bitter first-hand experience of mass surveillance under totalitarian regimes, the regulators have sharper teeth. Recently, Johannes Caspar, Hamburg's formidable commissioner for data protection, forced Google to suspend the transcription of voice recordings throughout the EU, while Apple and Facebook simultaneously halted transcription everywhere in the world. (Amazon merely allowed users to opt out of human monitoring.) The UK Information Commissioner's Office is investigating whether human oversight breaches the General Data Protection Regulation. "We have significant regulation in this area already, but the key is enforcement," says Veale. "Like all European data-protection authorities, the Information Commissioner's Office is underfunded and overstretched, and needs significant investment and support to protect citizens' fundamental rights."

Without effective regulation, there is no defence against more invasive exploitation of voice assistants. By definition always on, even when they are not awake, the devices are constantly listening, although not always transmitting. Gillula says that there are no technical obstacles to enabling dormant devices to, for example, track users' television viewing by responding to high-pitched signals embedded in shows and advertisements, or identify who is in the house at any given time. "That essentially becomes constant surveillance," Gillula says. "I am hopeful that the companies would never go down this dystopian path, but I could see them saying: 'Oh, it's a feature: know when your kids are home!' An appealing feature is how most of these things start."

Where they end up has galvanised not just privacy watchdogs but writers. The dystopian implications of voice assistants are appearing in science fiction, including the Spike Jonze movie Her, Black Mirror and Years and Years. Behind them all looms the "neversleeping ear" of George Orwell's telescreen in Nineteen Eighty-Four: "You had to live – did live, from habit that became instinct – in the assumption that every sound you made was overheard." The Echo Show, a smart assistant with a screen and camera, was widely compared to the telescreen when it was introduced two years ago. "Alexa, show me the dystopia," quipped Vice. In Joanna Kavenna's satirical novel Zed, the writer explores the "weird dysfunctional-servant aspect" of real-life voice assistants (which all have female voices as their default setting) and the sociopolitical consequences of the One Voice: in Zed, the tech monopoly, Beetle, is omnipresent and unaccountable. "The democratic idea is that we're meant to have transparent corporations and governments, while people have privacy," she says. "We have the inverse. People are uneasy because it's not being debated at a mature, democratic level."

Kavenna worries that, far from legislating to protect user privacy, US states will seek to access voice-assistant recordings in the name of crime prevention and national security. Last year, a judge in New Hampshire made headlines by ordering Amazon to submit Echo recordings of a double murder to investigators. "It puts them in a very complicated position between their customers and the government," Kavenna says. "We're very dependent on the political regime."

Rotenberg agrees: "If you're an authoritarian country, why not just run the audio stream straight to a government surveillance agency and argue that it's to reduce crime in the home? It's scary to contemplate, but conceivable."

Today, voice assistants are not the most pressing threat to privacy only because they are optional. A facial recognition scanner can spy on you in a public space, but Alexa, like a vampire, must be invited into your home. The only truly effective power you can wield over this technology is not to use it. But making an informed choice is compromised by misleading marketing and undermined by Amazon's efforts to embed Alexa into countless products, including cars, televisions, headphones, microwaves, thermostats and clocks, while signing deals with housebuilding companies and hotel chains, all with an eye to becoming the One Voice. "Voice control is being forced down consumers' throats whether they like it or not," says Estes.

We are not there yet. Tech companies rely on the myth of technological inevitability to occlude the business decisions they have made and the possibility of other models. To challenge them is to fight the future. Nonsense, says Kavenna. "Is it an inevitable consequence of tech? No, it's an ideological application of tech. If you build a building, you don't have to build a panopticon. It doesn't have to be what we have now. They'll often claim that if you're opposed to this, you're a neo-luddite. That myth has allowed a lot of people to become incredibly rich."

None of the people I spoke to owns a home voice assistant, nor would they advise anyone to get one, but they all agree that it would be possible to develop a device that delivers the most popular services while respecting the user's privacy. If the entire industry were to follow Apple's lead in making human monitoring opt-in rather than opt-out, that would be a strong start. Then, as processing power increases, more tasks could be performed inside the device. But, of course, that would mean forfeiting that juicy, monetisable data. "A lot of stuff that you really want to do shouldn't require the internet, and once you cut off access to the cloud, then the privacy concerns fade away," says Estes. "There's always the potential for things to get better – and there's always going to be a fight to get to that point."

Jeremy Gillula is so convinced that a safe, fully user-controlled voice assistant is possible that he is designing his own, using open-source software.

"I'm getting there," he says cheerfully. "I'm not 100% satisfied yet, but it will turn the lights on and off."

9 October 2019

Amazon Echo's privacy issues go way beyond voice recordings

An article from The Conversation.

By Garfield Benjamin, Postdoctoral Researcher, School of Media Arts and Technology, Solent University

Amazon Echo and the Alexa voice assistant have had widely publicised issues with privacy. Whether it is the amount of data they collect or the fact that they reportedly pay employees and, at times, external contractors from all over the world to listen to recordings to improve accuracy, the potential is there for sensitive personal information to be leaked through these devices.

But the risks extend not just to our relationship with Amazon. Major privacy concerns are starting to emerge in the way Alexa devices interact with other services – risking a dystopian spiral of increasing surveillance and control.

The setup of the Echo turns Amazon into an extra gateway that every online interaction has to pass through, collecting data on each one. Alexa knows what you are searching for, listening to or sending in your messages. Some smartphones do this already, particularly those made by Google and Apple who control the hardware, software and cloud services.

But the difference with an Echo is that it brings together the worst aspects of smartphones and smart homes. It is not a personal device but integrated into the home environment, always waiting to listen in. Alexa even features an art project (not created by Amazon) that tries to make light of this with the creepy "Ask the Listeners" function that makes comments about just how much the device is spying on you. Some Echo devices already have cameras, and if facial recognition capabilities were added we could enter a world of pervasive monitoring in our most private spaces, even tracked as we move between locations.

This technology gives Amazon a huge amount of control over your data, which has long been the aim of most of the tech giants. While Apple and Google – who face their own privacy issues – have similar voice assistants, they have at least made progress running the software directly on their devices so they won't need to transfer recordings of your voice commands to their servers. Amazon doesn't appear to be trying to do the same.

This is, in part, because of the firm's aggressive business model. Amazon's systems appear not just designed to collect as much data as they can but also to create ways of sharing it. So the potential issues run much deeper than Alexa listening in on private moments.

Sharing with law enforcement

One area of concern is the potential for putting the ears of law enforcement in our homes, schools and workplaces. Apple has a history of resisting FBI requests for user data, and Twitter is relatively transparent about reporting on how it responds to requests from governments.

But Ring, the internet-connected home-security camera company owned by Amazon, has a high-profile relationship with police that involves handing over user data. Even the way citizens and police communicate is increasingly monitored and controlled by Amazon.

This risks embedding a culture of state surveillance in Amazon's operations, which could have worrying consequences. We've seen numerous examples of law enforcement and other government bodies in democratic countries using personal data to spy on people, both in breach of the law and within it but for reasons that go far beyond the prevention of terrorism. This kind of mass surveillance also creates severe potential for discrimination, as it has been shown repeatedly to have a worse impact on women and minority groups.

If Amazon isn't willing to push back, it's not hard to imagine Alexa recordings being handed over to the requests of government employees and law enforcement officers who might be willing to violate the spirit or letter of the law. And given international intelligence-sharing agreements, even if you trust your own government, do you trust others?

In response to this issue, an Amazon spokesperson said: "Amazon does not disclose customer information in response to government demands unless we're required to do so to comply with a legally valid and blinding order. Amazon objects to overbroad or otherwise inappropriate demands as a matter of course.

"Ring customers decide whether to share footage in response to asks from local police investigating cases. Local police are not able to see any information related to which Ring users received a request and whether they declined to share or opt out of future requests." They added that although local police can access Ring's Neighbors app for reporting criminal and suspicious activity, they cannot see or access user account information.

Tracking health issues

Health is another area where Amazon appears to be attempting a takeover. The UK's National Health Service (NHS) has signed a deal for medical advice to be provided via the Echo. At face value, this simply extends ways of accessing publicly available information like the NHS website or phone line 111 – no official patient data is being shared.

But it creates the possibility that Amazon could start tracking what health information we ask for through Alexa, effectively building profiles of users' medical histories. This could be linked to online shopping suggestions, third-party ads for costly therapies, or even ads that are potentially

traumatic (think women who've suffered miscarriages being shown baby products).

An Amazon spokesperson said: "Amazon does not build customer health profiles based on interactions with nhs.uk content or use such requests for marketing purposes. Alexa does not have access to any personal or private information from the NHS."

The crudeness and glitches of algorithmic advertising would violate the professional and moral standards that health services strive to maintain. Plus it would be highly invasive to treat the data in the same way many Echo recordings are. Would you want a random external contractor to know you were asking for sexual health advice?

Transparency

Underlying these issues is a lack of real transparency. Amazon is disturbingly quiet, evasive and reluctant to act when it comes to tackling the privacy implications of their practices, many of which are buried deep within their terms and conditions or hard-to-find settings. Even tech-savvy users don't necessarily know the full extent of the privacy risks, and when privacy features are added, they often only make users aware after researchers or the press raise the issue. It is entirely unfair to place such a burden on users to find out and mitigate what these risks are.

So if you have an Echo in your home, what should you do? There are many tips available on how to make the device more private, such as setting voice recordings to automatically delete or limiting what data is shared with third parties. But smart tech is almost always surveillance tech, and the best piece of advice is not to bring one into your home.

In response to the main points of this article, an Amazon spokesperson told The Conversation:

At Amazon, customer trust is at the centre of everything we do and we take privacy and security very seriously. We have always believed that privacy has to be foundational and built in to every piece of hardware, software, and service that we create. From the beginning, we've put customers in control and always look for ways to make it even easier for customers to have transparency and control over their Alexa experience. We've introduced several privacy improvements including the option to have voice recordings automatically deleted after three or 18 months on an ongoing basis, the ability to ask Alexa to "delete what I just said" and "delete what I said today," and the Alexa Privacy Hub, a resource available globally that is dedicated to helping customers learn more about our approach to privacy and the controls they have. We'll continue to invent more privacy features on behalf of customers.

This article has been amended to make clear the "Ask the Listeners" function is an art project created by a third party.

21 January 2020

Zoom is not the worst, just getting the attention software deserves

The rise of scrutiny of Zoom is welcome evidence that privacy and security are valued and essential as our lives and interactions become increasingly virtual.

Key findings

♦ Zoom already had security challenges before the Coronavirus-caused lockdowns.

♦ Massive adoption of Zoom led to more scrutiny and exposure of privacy and security issues.

♦ Any software under the same scrutiny and without a strong focus on these features would have shown similar failures.

♦ Communications apps and services deserve this level of scrutiny.

♦ Investors, boards, and now customers must demand more from the entire industry.

A few weeks ago, its name would probably have been unknown to you. Amidst the covid-19 crisis and the lockdown it caused, Zoom has suddenly become the go-to tool for video chat and conference calling, whether it's a business meeting, a drink with friends, or a much needed moment with your family. This intense rise in use has been financially good to the company, but it also came with a hefty toll on its image and serious scrutiny on its privacy and security practices.

While Zoom already had a bit of history of security failures (one of which forced Apple to take global action to protect its customers from staying highly vulnerable), it is nothing compared to what the company is going through right now. From security vulnerabilities to privacy issues to questionable ethical decisions, the quantity and seriousness of problems that have been exposed in the past few weeks have rarely been matched.

Issues revealed about Zoom in the past 4 weeks:

♦ Privacy policy that allowed data collected during meeting be sold

♦ iOS app using Facebook's SDK and sending data to Facebook (an issue PI has highlighted previously on other apps)

♦ Attendee tracking feature (flagged and removed)

♦ MacOS install process was opaque in the modules it initialised (fixed)

♦ Zoom 0-day allowing remote execution on Windows (fixed)

♦ Data mining to display LinkedIn profile of users (feature disabled)

♦ Data leak of thousands of email addresses

♦ Easy to guess meeting IDs (following a pattern) leading to Zoombombing

♦ Pretending to use end-to-end encryption

♦ Usage of poorly implemented home made encryption

♦ Questionable call routing policies, for example via China

A long list of flaws... but not a surprising one

Yet, is this enough to say that Zoom is terrible software and that you, your company or your community should absolutely stay away from it? The answer is not that obvious.

Zoom certainly displayed questionable ethical choices and poor security practices. Most of the issues that have been reported highlight how the company focused on making easy-to-use software and dedicated little resources to make it secure or privacy-friendly. But the reality is that almost any software which hasn't paid crucial attention to privacy and security before being massively adopted would have run into similar issues.

Most private software is developed for a specific audience with a specific goal. And while security might be a key marketing argument in some contexts, it's not always the case. Same goes for privacy, which is too often targeted at a niche audience.

While Zoom reportedly had issues which would have been critical for any software, chances are that any video conference system which suddenly multiplies its user base by a factor of 20 (Zoom went from 10 to 200 millions users in 3 months) would have had flaws of their own revealed. It's also important to flag that there are a great variety of use cases, from online classes to talking to your lawyer, and that one-size-fits-all solutions don't exist.

Software isn't the problem, our approach to developing it is

So what's wrong with Zoom then? How can a company which already had millions of users fail on so many levels? To put it simply, Zoom was developed as a business-to-business software with the wrong priorities in mind, and the attention it received is revealing poor development choices.

Prioritising frictionless use over privacy and security might seem a good idea when trying to enter the market and find new customers. In itself, it's not bad to focus on those things, but it should never be done at the expense of security and privacy.

Considerable financial investment has gone into Zoom – and it is alarming that neither the board nor investors brought these issues to the fore sooner. We hope that investment will encourage Zoom to follow sound security and privacy choices in the future.

Private software development is also guided by rapid release of features and bug fixes to maintain user satisfaction and in order to maximise profits. These were likely additional reasons to overlook security and privacy. User-facing features are often more appreciated by businesses than core security design or company ethos, making it tempting for companies to ignore those key features.

Privacy and security: core supporters of our humanity

In today's landscape, privacy and security cannot be considered optional. Today everyone is using services like Zoom: governments, schools, medical practices, law firms, journalists, families, friends, justice and rights groups like our own. No trustworthy service should place these people at risk. Somehow the UK Government Cabinet meetings still occur over Zoom despite concerns from the UK's Ministry of Defence, even as schools in New York and Singapore have moved away from the platform. Google and SpaceX staff are no longer allowed to either, nor the German government's foreign ministry.

All these problems could have and should have been caught earlier. In the EU and under GDPR, companies have to produce Data Protection Impact Assessments to justify and review their data collection, processing and protection practices. Although Zoom might be an American company, its user base is international (including European citizens) which make these sorts of practices necessary.

On the security side, a business-oriented company which provides communication channels should have a big focus on its security and undergo regular security audits.

When your customers include valuable organisations who are likely targets of foreign states and other actors, good security should be a fundamental promise. This is something some governments have already acknowledged, and mass adoption of business ready software should not be a problem if proper attention is given to security and privacy.

Those things should not be wishful thinking, they are critical elements to create strong and reliable communications technology that protects users. In the case of Zoom, they should be even more important given its initial focus on businesses. Now under fire, Zoom has made fixes and improvements to some critical issues, but there is still a lot to do to make the software secure by default, starting with a modification to the default settings and more transparency about the real software capabilities.

There is a lesson for all of us here: if this crisis is an opportunity to develop or improve our communication technologies, both security and privacy must be given the attention they deserve – that we deserve. The past weeks have highlighted how vital technologies can become in times where contact with each other is paramount to our mental health. If anything, Zoom's case has made more obvious that security and privacy are not optional but what people truly need. They are the fundamental layers that give us the peace of mind to reach out to others and let our humanity express itself.

21 April 2020

Apple's Siri violated 'the privacy of millions', says whistleblower

In 2019 news broke that Apple contractors were listening to users' Siri recordings without their knowledge or consent, but the company 'has not been subject to any kind of investigation'.

By Adam Smith

The whistleblower who exposed in 2019 that Apple contractors listened to users' Siri recordings without their knowledge or consent has gone public to protest the lack of action taken against the technology giant.

In a letter, sent to all European data protection regulators, Thomas le Bonniec said that Apple had conducted a "massive violation of the privacy of millions of citizens."

He wrote that although news of the case had already gone public, the technology giant "has not been subject to any kind of investigation to the best of my knowledge."

Mr Le Bonniec, who was hired by one of Apple's subcontractors in Ireland called Globe Technical Services, had to listen to recordings from users and correct transcription errors. Listening to hundreds of recordings from Apple's iPhones, iPads, and Apple Watches, many of them were taken "outside of any activation of Siri" – meaning that users were not aware of the action.

As well as recording their owners, Apple's devices also picked up speech involving relatives or children of the owners who divulged names, addresses, messages, searches, arguments, and conversations without their knowledge that it was being recorded.

This covered personal information, including "cancer, referring to dead relatives, religion, sexuality, pornography, politics, school, relationships, or drugs," Mr le Bonniec said.

The letter also stated that workers on another project, "Development data," also had access to these recordings. This project entailed tagging words in the recordings to be linked to user data. This includes phone contacts, locations, or music.

"In other words, staff assigned to the project had access to personal user information, and used it to be able to link it to Siri commands. This means that users' playlists, contact details, notes, calendars, photos, maps, etc. were gathered in huge data sets, ready to be exploited by Apple for other projects," the letter stated.

In August 2019, as a response to this news, the Cupertino company fired 300 workers with only one week's notice and said it was reviewing its audio program. Mr Le Bonniec said that "nothing has been done to verify if Apple actually stopped the program," with sources reportedly telling him that Apple has not taken action.

Apple touts its privacy practices compared to competitors such as Google, but has often been criticised for using such principles as a marketing tool, especially on political grounds.

"I believe that Apple's statements merely aim to reassure their users and public authorities, and they do not care for their user's consent, unless being forced to obtain it by law" Mr le Bonniec wrote.

When asked for comment, Apple directed us to its August Newsroom post from 2019 and its Ask Siri Dictation & Privacy support page.

We have reached out to the company for a statement.

20 May 2020

The perils of 'sharenting': The parents who share too much

By the age of five, many children will have had 1,500 photos of them shared online. But what happens when they grow up?

By Rosie Hopegood

David Devore Jr is just like any other 18-year-old. On Instagram, he posts pictures with his prom date and of his college acceptance letter. On Twitter, he tweets about his favourite football team and shares clips from TikTok stars. But there is one thing that sets him apart from other kids his age: On YouTube, there is a video of him, aged seven, which has amassed almost 140 million views.

In 2009, David Jr, who lives in Florida, became one of the world's first viral video stars when his dad, David Sr, uploaded a YouTube video of him, dazed and delirious, after a routine tooth extraction with the unassuming title: David After Dentist.

"I just wanted to be able to share it with friends and family because it made us laugh – David Jr included," says David Sr. "I didn't think anyone else would click on it."

But, within days, it had been watched more than four million times, and the numbers continued to rise.

David Jr was so popular he was flown around the world to appear on talk shows and on red carpets. But there was also a darker side to the attention. "People were accusing me of child abuse," says David Sr. "One reporter said the police should be called and I should go to jail. They were attacking who I was as a parent."

The Devore family's story is a cautionary tale – albeit an extreme one – that once a child's image is posted online, it is not easy to control where it goes. David Jr is part of the first generation of children to reach adulthood who are inheriting a digital footprint that they had no say in creating. According to a recent UK study, the average parent will post online 1,500 pictures of their child before the age of five. Almost a third of parents surveyed said they had never thought to seek a child's permission before posting.

'Sharenting'

While David Jr says the video has been a "positive thing" in his life and is pleased that the six-figure sum his family earned is helping to pay for his college, there is growing unease among Generation Z about the online legacy their parents are handing them.

When Gwyneth Paltrow posted an Instagram selfie on a ski lift with her 14-year-old daughter, Apple, last year, a rather public tiff ensued. "Mom, we have discussed this. You may not post anything without my consent," Apple wrote.

It is a problem being echoed around the world. Last year, Microsoft released the results of an internet safety study of 12,500 teens across 25 countries. Of the teens surveyed, 42 percent said they were distressed about how much their parents "sharented" online, with 11 percent of them believing it was a "big problem" in their lives.

Earlier this year, the child of an Instagram influencer wrote an anonymous Reddit post vocalising concerns about the images posted by their mother. "It sucks because there's so much out there about us and it's what's gonna come up when I'm looking for a job, when I'm dating, when anyone looks up my name," wrote the user, before detailing a plan to stop the mother being able to take pictures: wearing hoodies printed with slogans such as, "I do not consent to be photographed" and "No profiting off my image". "I know it's really weird looking but it feels like my only option," the user concluded.

According to Stacey Steinberg, a law professor at the University of Florida and author of Growing Up Shared: How Parents Can Share Smarter on Social Media and What You Can Do To Keep Your Family Safe in a No-Privacy World, younger people are right to be wary of "sharenting".

"Once a picture's out there, it's out there. There's a meme of a chubby, naked toddler, with a caption about overeating for the holidays," she says. "I did a reverse image search and found that that image had been shared thousands of times. How will this child feel when they find out that they were made a public joke? Thirty years from now, the facial recognition technology may exist to pair that naked toddler image with a CEO, for example."

As well as the scope for embarrassment, there is also the potential for damage to relationships between parents and their children. "Teenagers may become resentful to their parents," says Yair Cohen, a UK-based lawyer who specialises in social media. "The issue of self-image is very significant at this age – this is a time when they might not like their bodies or the way they are portrayed in photographs. In the end, they may think, 'Why did you do this to me? You're meant to protect me but actually, you exposed me.'"

Adolescent therapist Robert Batt, who runs clinics in Riyadh and London, agrees: "Our job really is to think about the feelings of the adolescent. It's important to make sure those feelings are respected, because if they aren't, then we'll start seeing consequences. What is more important: the ego and image of the parent, or the feelings of the child who's being used as a tool?"

Future legal cases

In an era where it is common to share photographs of a baby while it is still in the womb and "mumfluencers" represent an $11bn industry, just what is the future of sharenting?

Could a young person, upset by what they see as a breach of their privacy, take legal action against their parents?

"All the way around the world, people are talking about sharenting," says Claire Bessant, an associate professor at Northumbria Law School, who is currently working on a project examining the legal protections for children of British "sharents".

"But actually, no one has brought a case to court yet. There are legal remedies, but all of them would be really setting the parents and the child up in this huge court battle. If they won, they might get the pictures taken down. But what damage would that do to the relationship?"

Bessant's interest in sharenting piqued in 2016 after a story published in an Austrian magazine was republished around the world. The story, which was later debunked, detailed the case of an 18-year-old girl who was suing her parents after discovering 500 childhood photos of her on their Facebook pages. The young woman was quoted as saying her parents "knew no shame" and that "every step of [her life] had been photographically recorded and subsequently made public". Although the court case turned out to be fake, Bessant believes it is only a matter of time before a child does launch legal proceedings against their parents.

Attitudes to sharenting vary from country to country. In 2015, German police ran a social media campaign warning parents against posting pictures of their children publicly on Facebook because paedophiles can use the images nefariously.

The following year, French lawyers warned that a child could grow up to sue their parents for risking their security. Under strict privacy laws, parents could face a year in jail or a $45,000 fine. "The French have opened a window here for something to happen a few years' time," says Cohen.

"There could be pictures being taken today that will at some point potentially be the basis of future court action and if

this happens, the parents will need to be able to explain how those pictures were published in the child's best interests. The signs are there that in liberal Europe there will be changes in the law sooner or later because there is a human rights issue here."

A backlash

If it is an issue for regular kids, then it is an even bigger one for the offspring of parents who blog about their families. In the US alone, 3.9 million mothers identify as bloggers.

As the children of these so-called "influencers" grow up, the likelihood of potential for legal proceedings increases.

"There's going to be a backlash as this generation comes of age and attempts to assert their own autonomy," says Steinberg. "With a digital identity and a personality not of their own making, some of them aren't going to be too thrilled with what was created for them. I've gone through a lot of iterations as I've grown into myself, but if I search my name on Google, the results are either things I put there myself or things which happened because of my actions, rather than those of my parents."

The complexity of this situation is not lost on Irish blogger Karen Edwards, who has more than 103,000 followers on Instagram and runs the successful blog, Travel Mad Mum. Karen's blog has enabled her family to travel all over the world for free, staying in luxury hotels in exotic locations in return for coverage. "Starting out as a blogger, I thought, 'Wow, this is awesome – we're giving the kids these amazing opportunities we couldn't otherwise afford.' But at the same time, my child is being used as an ad, and I do have that in the back of my mind. I think about posing this to my daughter as an adult: would you want to have this amazing experience or would you prefer not to have your face on the internet? It's difficult as she isn't really able to consent – at the age of five, she isn't old enough to fully understand."

Because parental blogging is relatively new, there are very few regulations in place regarding the use of children in sponsored posts. Blandine Poidevin, associate lawyer and founder of Jurisexpert, a French law firm that specialises in IT law, notes that in France the law has not caught up with technology.

"If a child appears in a traditional advert, the money earned must be held in a trust fund for the child rather than being spent by the parent," she says. "The rules about this are very strict, but these rules are not applied when it comes to social media. I'm sure that in the next few years, we will have claims from children who will ask for the money their parents have made."

Blandine's firm has already dealt with several court cases in which divorced parents disagree about images of their child being posted online. In May this year, a Dutch grandmother was ordered by a court to delete photographs of her grandchild on Facebook and Pinterest after the child's mother launched legal action. The ruling stated the photographs posted on Facebook made them available to a wide audience and "it cannot be ruled out that placed photos may be distributed and may end up in the hands of third parties".

Dark uses

This lesson was learned the hard way by American mother Laney Griner when she posted a picture of her 11-month-old son Sam on Flickr in 2007. Something about the expression on Sam's face as he fist-pumped on a beach captured the internet's attention, and the photograph became the widely shared meme, "Success Kid". The meme is so popular it is still being shared 13 years on, and, in January of this year, the Griner family's lawyers issued a cease and desist letter to far-right politician Steve King after the image was used in a fundraising advertisement. "Just so it's clear," Griner tweeted. "I have/would never give permission for use of my son's photo to promote any agenda of this vile man or that disgusting party."

Viral fame such as that found by David Devore Jr and Sam Griner is, of course, uncommon. But cases such as these highlight how difficult it is to maintain control of an online image.

While most children's photographs will not go viral, they could be used in unintended ways. In 2018, UK bank Barclays warned that parents are putting their children at risk of fraud by sharing photographs and information about their children online. By 2030, the bank forecasts that 670 million pounds ($867m) worth of fraud could stem from details shared by parents. "From a parent's social media, third parties can figure out a child's name, date of birth, where they live," says Steinberg. "We know that companies are creating digital dossiers on us – what if they're creating digital identities for our kids? We are shepherds of our children's personal information – we're supposed to keep their information safe."

There is another, darker way that children's photographs are sometimes used. In 2015, Australian investigators found more than 45 million photos of children engaged in everyday activities on paedophile image-sharing sites. The photos had been downloaded from social media sites and family blogs.

Abigail Caidoy, a Dubai-based "mummy blogger" who runs the popular site, Cuddles and Crumbs, became concerned about how photos of her children could be misappropriated after reading similar reports. "It made me stop and think," she says. "My husband and I talked it through, and I went through old blog posts and removed photos of my sons that I no longer felt comfortable sharing – baby photos or ones without shirts."

Caidoy grew up in the Philippines and is struck by the differing attitudes to sharenting there and in the United Arab Emirates. "A lot of the mommy bloggers that I know here post snaps of their children without including their face, just the back of their heads," she says. "In the Middle East, people are more careful of photos being shared. But in the Philippines, everything is documented. Every month, there would be photoshoots celebrating the child's milestones and these would be shared publicly."

Changing childhood

With such an abundance of childhood imagery now being produced, future historians will be facing a very different profession. "Social history is going to be vastly different," says Ellen Smith, a PhD candidate at the University of Leicester whose work focuses on family histories in the 19th century. "Even with the boom in recording and writing in the 19th century, it's often still a huge task even to find information about our ancestors.

"Now, there's more of a platform for everyone to project their own identities, which is liberating in a way, but it does bring into question the profession of a historian. Our cultural identity could become blurred because there is so much information being produced and it might be too much to process."

With social media and the widespread use of camera phones still relatively new in technology terms, it is modern-day sharenting that has yet to be judged by generations to come.

At the heart of it all lies a question: Whose stories are these to tell? Steinberg urges caution: "If we keep curating childhood through our social media posts, kids won't remember what it feels like to actually be a child – what it feels like to be on stage doing that dance, or what it feels like to see Mickey Mouse for the first time. They're only going to see it through our eyes through the selected pictures that we posted online."

11 October 2020

Is sharing photos of children fun – or a dangerous invasion of privacy?

'Mom, we have discussed this. You may not post anything without my consent'

By Chloe Hamilton

You might not be able to make out her face in the photo, obscured as it is by a pair of enormous skiing goggles, but the caption – apple, skiing and heart emojis – suggested that the picture uploaded to Gwyneth Paltrow's Instagram page this week was of her daughter, Apple Martin.

It was the 14-year-old who cleared up any lingering doubt, writing snippily beneath the picture: "Mom, we have discussed this. You may not post anything without my consent."

Paltrow, whose picture of her daughter garnered more than 150,000 likes, is not the first to come a cropper when it comes to "sharenting" – parents' overuse of social media content based on their children – although she is certainly the most high-profile example to have been called out on it in such a public way.

It is an issue that affects celebrity parents, Instagram influencers and regular mums and dads alike.

Digital footprint

A child's digital footprint begins as early as in the womb, with many expecting parents posting photos of their scan on their social media profiles by way of sharing their happy news.

Pictures of births, first steps, first days at school, and academic achievements follow, all shared with friends and followers, unbeknown to the children in question who are, often, not old enough to understand the knock-on effects of having a digital footprint let alone to consent to having one.

According to the Office of the Children's Commissioner for England, by the age of 13, there are more than 1,000 pictures of the average child on the internet.

"There is a discrepancy between what parents and their children consider good and cute photos to share." - Professor Andra Siibak

But sharenting has become increasingly divisive. What might have started as harmless fun has, arguably, become a dangerous and damaging invasion of privacy. Andra Siibak, a professor in media studies at the University of Tartu in Estonia, has carried out research into the matter and says that although the impact on children is not yet fully understood – the phenomenon itself is still relatively new – one study which involved Estonian children aged between nine and 13 showed that pre-teens in particular struggle with it.

"Our study of sharenting suggests that children have nothing against it in cases of parents sharing things that reflect positively on their self-image, such as doing well in school or in sports, and photos reflecting happy family life," she says.

"But there is a discrepancy between what parents and their children consider good and cute photos to share. Pre-teens want to voice their opinions, to have parents discuss these issues with them before sharenting."

Cause of anxiety

For teenagers struggling with self-image issues, photos shared online by love-blind parents can cause anxiety if they are perceived by the young subject to be unflattering or embarrassing.

"When I saw the pictures that she (my mum) had been posting on Facebook for years, I felt utterly embarrassed, and deeply betrayed." -Teenager Sonia Bokhari

"If we think about how self-conscious young people can feel and how they're trying to find their own identity, I think having things put online all the time can be quite challenging for them," says Dr Catherine Hamilton-Giachritsis, from the Department of Psychology at the University of Bath. "On the one hand it can seem like a nice record but on the other hand, you're removing that child's right to decide for themselves."

Sonia Bokhari, 14, from the US, recently wrote an article in the business magazine Fast Company on the issue. Sonia, who has since left social media, signed up to Twitter and Facebook when she turned 13 and only then realised that her mum and sister had been posting about her for her entire life.

"When I saw the pictures that she (my mum) had been posting on Facebook for years, I felt utterly embarrassed, and deeply betrayed."

"There, for anyone to see on her public Facebook account, were all of the embarrassing moments from my childhood: the letter I wrote to the tooth fairy when I was five, pictures of me crying when I was a toddler, and even vacation pictures of me when I was 12 and 13 that I had no knowledge of. It seemed that my entire life was documented on her Facebook account, and for 13 years, I had no idea."

An overreaction?

But are we overreacting? Maybe sharing photos of offspring is simply a modern way of showing parental love. Perhaps Ms Paltrow simply couldn't resist showing the world the apple

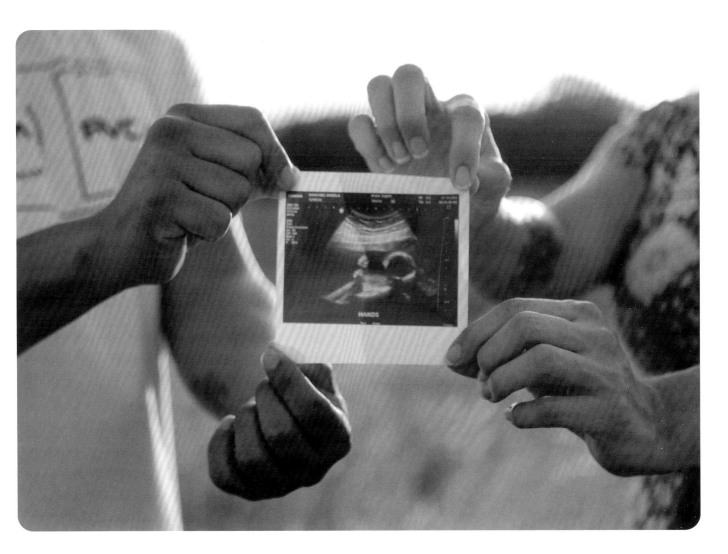

of her eye. Not to mention the fact that celebrity children who regularly appear on their parents' Instagram pages as part of the family – think of the Beckhams – presumably benefit from the exposure.

The brand brings in the big bucks. The big bucks pay for private education, horse-riding lessons, ski trips and more. Is giving up their digital privacy the price such children have to pay?

According to Professor Siibak, many young parents are now "digital natives" and have a greater understanding of the risks involved in online oversharing, including "digital kidnapping" – when strangers take publicly available photos of children and use them for sinister purposes. Research by Barclays suggests that, by 2030, information shared by parents online will lead to two-thirds of the identity theft committed against young people.

"Many young mothers are increasingly concerned and feel charged upon for engaging in sharenting." - Professor Andra Siibak

Professor Siibak recently interviewed mothers in their early to mid-20s with children aged from birth to three. "They had experienced problems in their youth due to the internet, such as identity theft, their photos being used in other contexts, or had friends with such problems," she says. "They are more cautious now with the digital footprint of their own children."

The same study showed that as sharenting gains an increasingly negative reputation, some parents are finding they can't share any photos of their children online for fear of exposing themselves to a backlash. "Many young mothers are increasingly concerned and feel charged upon for engaging in sharenting," says Professor Siibak. "At the same time, however, they feel sad when not sharing, as it is like hiding an important part of their identity."

Perhaps it is simply time parents stepped into the shoes of their children. "I think it would be good for parents to think about how they would feel if somebody took a video of them – maybe if they were having a meltdown, as we all do at some point – and put it on social media," says Dr Hamilton-Giachritsis. "If people could apply that a little bit more to themselves, maybe they would make slightly different decisions."

29 March 2019, updated 15 October 2020.

- Prediction: 65% of people across the world will have their personal data protected by privacy regulations in 2021, compared to 10% in 2020. (page 2)

- In 2019 it was estimated the number of smart speakers worldwide was set to reach 225 million by 2020, despite multiple incidents of speakers recording private conversations and sending them to acquaintances without the user's knowledge. (page 7)

- In 2018, the European Union rolled out the General Data Protection Regulation (GDPR) — the largest attempt yet at protecting user data. (page 7)

- The 2018 California Consumer Privacy Protection law is the strongest privacy law in the US. It guarantees users the right to know what data is being collected, and opting out of the sale of their data. (page 7)

- The Chinese government collects personal data from citizens to build a social credit system to incentivise good behaviour. (page 7)

- The projected growth of IoT devices is staggering. By 2025, they're expected to reach 75.44 billion – an increase of 146% from 2020. (page 10)

- Your privacy is interwoven with that of others. Take the Cambridge Analytica scandal. Only 270,000 Facebook users consented to the firm collecting their data. The other 87 million people were the friends of those consenting users, and their data was harvested without their knowledge or consent. (page 11)

- The Investigatory Powers Act 2016 formalised existing capabilities of the security services such as phone tapping or collecting bulk communications data. (page 17)

- In May 2020, the company Facewatch announced they had developed a new form of facial recognition technology that allows for the identification of individuals based solely on the eye region, between the cheekbones and the eyebrows. (page 18)

- Article 8 of the European Convention on Human Rights outlines rights to privacy. (page 21)

- Under the General Data Protection Regulation (GDPR) every project which involves people's data must first conduct a Data Protection Impact Assessment (DPIA) on privacy. (page 22)

- The UK government's coronavirus test and trace scheme which involves those infected with Covid-19 passing on personal information and the details of those they have been in contact with, was launched in May 2020. No DPIA was carried out beforehand. (page 22)

- There are three kinds of relationships in an Internet of Things (IoT) network: things-things, people-things and people-people. (page 24)

- Amazon released the Echo in the US in 2014. Dot, the Echo's cheaper, smaller model, was launched in 2016. (page 26)

- In January 2019, Amazon revealed that the company had sold more than 100m Alexa-enabled devices. Last year in the US, where one in five adults own a home voice assistant, Alexa had a 70% US market share, compared with the Google Assistant's 24%. (page 26)

- Voice recognition didn't become commonplace until Apple launched its phone-based voice assistant, Siri, in 2011. (page 27)

- Zoom went from 10 to 200 million users in 3 months in 2020 due to the covid-19 crisis and the lockdown it caused. (page 32)

- In 2019, Microsoft released the results of an internet safety study of 12,500 teens across 25 countries. Of the teens surveyed, 42 percent said they were distressed about how much their parents "sharented" online, with 11 percent of them believing it was a "big problem" in their lives. (page 35)

- The UK bank Barclays forecasts that by 2030, 670 million pounds ($867m) worth of fraud could stem from details shared by parents (about their children). (page 37)

- In 2015, Australian investigators found more than 45 million photos of children engaged in everyday activities on paedophile image-sharing sites. The photos had been downloaded from social media sites and family blogs. (page 37)

- According to the Office of the Children's Commissioner for England, by the age of 13, there are more than 1,000 pictures of the average child on the internet. (page 38)

Article 8: Right to privacy

Article 8 of the European Convention on Human Rights states that 'Everyone has the right to respect for his private and family life, his home and his correspondence.' There are some exceptions to this rule, however, so this means that your right to privacy can be interfered with as long as it is 'in accordance with law' and 'necessary in a democratic society'.

Big Brother

The term comes from a character in George Orwell's novel Nineteen Eighty-Four, from which the phrase 'Big Brother is watching you originated. Big Brother emobodied totalitarianism; a regime where the government controls and monitors every aspect of people's lives and behaviour.

Biometric data

Biometrics (or biometric authentification) refers to a method of uniquely identifying people. This includes methods such as fingerprints, DNA, retinal scans (eyes) and facial recognition; something that is permanent throughout a person's lifetime and doesn't change as they age. The main uses of biometric data are for the purpose of controlling access (e.g. some laptops have fingerprint scanners) or helping tackle and prevent crime.

CCTV

Closed-circuit television (CCTV) is the use of mounted video cameras which broadcast a live image to a television screen closely watched over by someone (can be recorded). CCTV is used to observe an area in an effort to reduce and prevent crime. However, the use of CCTV has triggered a debate about security versus privacy.

Data Protection Act 2018

The Data Protection Act controls how your personal information is used by organisations, businesses or the government. The Data Protection Act 2018 is the UK's implementation of the General Data Protection Regulation (GDPR).

DNA database/United Kingdom National DNA Database

In 1995, the UK established a national database of DNA profiles which the police can use to match suspect DNA. Samples are taken from crime scenes, police suspects and anyone arrested and detained at a police station (in England and Wales). The database has helped in solving both past and present crimes. However, controversial privacy issues about the DNA database have arisen because samples have been taken and held on to from people who are innocent and some people feel that they should be removed/destroyed from the database. In 2020 it was estimated to contain 6.6 million profiles (5.6 million individuals excluding duplicates).

Facial recognition

Facial recognition is a method of identification using biometric software to map, analyse and confirm the identity of a face in photograph or video. It is also a powerful surveillance tool.

GDPR (General Data Protection Regulation)

The GDPR is a legal framework setting guidelines for the collecting and processing of personal information from individuals who live in the European Union. It is the toughest privacy and security law in the world.

Protection of Freedoms Act 2012

An act that regulates the use of biometric data, the use of surveillance and many other things. For example, this will mean schools need to get parents' consent before processing a child's biometric information and it also introduces a code of practice for surveillance camera systems. Essentially, this is to help protect people from state intrusion in their lives.

Surveillance

The close observation and monitoring of behaviour or activities. To keep watch over a person or a group. The UK has been described as a 'surveillance society' because of its large number of CCTV cameras and the national DNA database; the UK was once referred to as 'the most surveilled country' in the Western states.

.

Activities

Brainstorming

- In small groups, discuss what you know about privacy:

  - What is the 'right to privacy'?

  - What types of privacy are there?

  - Give some examples of breaches of privacy.

  - What is GDPR?

Research

- Look up Article 8 of the European Convention of Human Rights – Right to respect for private and family life, home and correspondence. Can you think of any situations in your own experience where this right has not been observed? Can you also think of any high-profile cases in the news, where a famous person has had their right to privacy ignored? Share the examples you have found with the rest of your study group.

- Investigate how views and laws regarding privacy in the UK compare to those in one of the following countries:

  - United States

  - China

  - UAE

  - India

- In small groups do some research into surveillance drones. Do you think they are an invasion of privacy, an important tool for law enforcement or a useful means of information-gathering? Can you find examples reported in the news where use of surveillance drones has been an asset, and where it has been a liability? Feedback your findings to the rest of the class.

- Choose a partner. Using the internet, research your partner from the persepective of someone who doesn't already know them and write down what you find out about them. You could try typing their name into a search engine and have a look at social media sites. How much information have you found? How easy/difficult was it? Do you think your partner takes enough care with their online safety? Give them some feedback.

Design

- Choose one of the articles from this book and create an illustration to highlight the key themes of the piece.

- Created by the Council of Europe in 2006, Data Privacy Day, also known as Data Protection Day, is celebrated every year on 28 January. Design a series of posters and web-banners to advertise it.

- Design an infographic that demonstrates the key aspects of 'Freedom of Information'.

- Design a piece of wearable technology that a firm could use to track their employees' actions. Think about what kind of things employers would want to keep an eye on, e.g. use of work email, internet use and amount of time spent away from desk.

- Create a poster illustrating some of the consequences of not protecting your privacy online.

Oral

- Create a digital presentation arguing that smart technology such as Smart TVs are a dangerous step towards invasion of privacy. Share with your class.

- In small groups, think about what you would tell someone who has just started using the internet and social media about how they should guard their privacy. Make a bullet point list and share with the rest of your class.

- In pairs, discuss how you feel about the following surveillance technologies. Are they a good thing or an invasion of privacy?

  - CCTV

  - Facial recognition

Reading/writing

- Write a short story about what the future would be like if a government who abused technology such as facial recognition, ID cards and the DNA database came to power. How might they use these things to control citizens? What would life be like for people living in this future society? Your story should be around 700 –1000 words.

- Write a short paragraph definition of the following:

  - Privacy

  - Surveillance

  - The Internet of Things.

- Imagine you are a teenager who has just realised their parents or another family member have been sharing photos of them online for years without their knowledge. How do you feel about it? Do you think it's a gross breach of your personal privacy, or are you not really bothered? Write a blogpost explaining your reaction to it.

Acknowledgements

The publisher is grateful for permission to reproduce the material in this book. While every care has been taken to trace and acknowledge copyright, the publisher tenders its apology for any accidental infringement or where copyright has proved untraceable. The publisher would be pleased to come to a suitable arrangement in any such case with the rightful owner.

The material reproduced in *ISSUES* books is provided as an educational resource only. The views, opinions and information contained within reprinted material in *ISSUES* books do not necessarily represent those of Independence Educational Publishers and its employees.

Images

Cover image courtesy of iStock. All other images courtesy of Pixabay and Unsplash except for page 31 - image by Christos S from www.shutterstock.com

Icons

Icons on pages 24, 25 & 34 were made by Dinosoftlabs, freepik, itim2101, Pixelperfect, srip, surang, & Ultimatearm from www.flaticon.com.

Illustrations

Simon Kneebone: pages 7, 21 & 36. Angelo Madrid: pages 1, 19 & 33.

Additional acknowledgements

With thanks to the Independence team: Shelley Baldry, Danielle Lobban, Jackie Staines and Jan Sunderland.

Tracy Biram

Cambridge, January 2021